COMMON PHRASES AND WHERE THEY COME FROM

COMMON PHRASES AND WHERE THEY COME FROM

Myron Korach

in Collaboration with

John B. Mordock

THE LYONS PRESS
Guilford, CT
An Imprint of Globe Pequot Press

The Lyons Press is an imprint of The Globe Pequot Press.

Library of Congress Cataloging-in-Publication Data
Korach, Myron.
    Common phrases and where they come from / Myron Korach, in col-
laboration with John B. Mordock.
    p. cm.
    ISBN 1-58574-218-X
    1. English language—Etymology. 2. English language—Terms and
phrases. I. Mordock, John B. II. Title.

PE1574 .K67 2001
422—dc21

                                                              00-069016

Printed in the United States of America

10 9 8 7 6 5 4 3 2 1

Contents

Preface

The purpose of this book is neither just to entertain—although many of the idioms have entertaining, if not humorous, origins—nor just to inform, although its contents are informative. The real purpose is to acquaint you with some of your own history; a history we all share no matter what our station in life. More specifically, we want to make you aware of the historical circumstances that produced today's brief, colorful phrases that convey powerful meanings; to illustrate the way our language is shaped by our past history and how this history influences our current communications. While some idioms arose following significant historical events, most came out of the everyday lives of common folks.

Typically we use idioms in our conversations or writings without realizing that they don't make sense if taken literally. We fail to understand that others, unfamiliar with them, will be confused by their use. If you repeatedly criticize an idea in a consensus-building meeting, for instance, and someone reminds you that "anyone can kick a barn," those unfamiliar with idioms will think the speaker has "gone batty." And others, unfamiliar with the specific idiom, will have no idea what the speaker is talking about but may be reluctant to ask exactly what she means.

But without idioms our language would be boring. Idioms not only "dress up" or "dress down" (depending on the situation) our language but give some spice to it as well. While we use idioms constantly, very few of us realize that each has its own unique origin. They just didn't appear spontaneously; they have a history, and each of these histories is worth knowing. The histories tell us something about ourselves—who we are and where we came from.

Because we want to inform as well as entertain, we've made no effort to trace the origin of *every* idiom in current use. While there are perhaps thousands of such phrases, the origins of many are of little historical interest. For example, "top banana"—our title for chapter 9—evolved from an audience's view of stage dancers from a distance; they looked like a line of bananas, with the lead dancer being the "top banana." But this story contributes little to an understanding of our etymological history, so we decided not to include the origins of those idioms whose histories were rather unremarkable. We did, though, discover many phrases whose histories were surprisingly humorous.

Our introduction is devoted to a discussion of idioms in general and how we went about developing this book. Here we would like to acknowledge some sources and some individuals who contributed to our efforts. First, because idioms were his hobby and not his academic passion, Myron Korach, who traced the origin of the majority of idioms in this book, did not keep track of the exact sources where an idiom's history revealed itself.

Preface

Using public library archives, both in his home state and during his travels, he found the histories primarily in old magazine articles and books. The British magazine *Puck* was the source for many. Others were found in old novels or in books on mercantile, maritime, and military history. Some of the histories could be partially substantiated by examining general references, such as the twenty-two-thousand-page *Oxford English Dictionary,* but many could not.

In his initial foray into researching the origin of idioms, Myron was assisted by a colleague and close friend. In 1942, Henry Hertz, a practicing attorney now deceased, edited a selection of Myron's idioms that were scheduled for presentation over the airwaves. Billy Hillpot, moderator of an NBC show called *Information Please,* had read some of the histories in Myron's collection and thought they would be of interest to his listeners. The two lawyers, Hertz and Korach, now aspiring scriptwriters, paid a one-dollar fee to the Screen Writers' Guild, affiliated at that time with the Authors' League of America, to copyright the material (Screen Writers' Guild, Inc., No. 26982, "Phrase Origins"). Unfortunately, two significant but unrelated events occurred: The Japanese bombed Pearl Harbor, and some structural changes took place within NBC. As a result, the presentation never materialized. Nevertheless, we would like to acknowledge Henry Hertz for his early efforts.

We would like to thank our closest loved ones for their patience with us during our work and for their willingness to listen to our "ranting and raving" about an idiom's roots whether they were interested or not.

Hammer Out

An idiom or common phrase is a speech form or expression that cannot be understood from the individual meaning of its elements. Such phrases are in use all around us every day. Samuel Langhorne Clemens, known by most of us as Mark Twain, took his pen name from the idiom "mark twain," a command "barked out" by Mississippi riverboat captains to their boatmen. It was a request to mark the river's depth as they traveled upstream in uncharted waters.

Idioms are in daily use by people in "all walks of life." You don't have to look far to find them. For example, in a column by Alan Abelson titled *Down Wall Street,* which appeared in the October 19, 1998, issue of *Barron's,* he used twenty-eight idioms to discuss a recent federal increase in the interest rates:

> Hell in a handbasket
> Sixes and sevens
> Scared stiff
> Getting a charge

Risen the ranks of the saviors
Bucked the trend
Turns of misfortune's screw
Wiseacres of the whisper circuit
Had it cold
Step on the odd banana peel
Shotgun marriage
Feeling some pain
Render the rumor crowd mute
Add fuel to the fire
Patch up the leaks
Speaking his mind
Nip in the bud
Clear as crystal
Keeps close tabs
Pink slip
Wield their hatchets
Vicious circle
Picks up steam
Doesn't stack up
What goes around comes around
Spread-eagled
Black holes in the cosmos
In the fullness of time

Even the title of Abelson's article, "Prozac Fix," could be considered an idiom in the manner that it was used.

While some might say that Mr. Abelson is "big on" or "has a thing for" idioms, closer examination of that same

October 19 issue reveals that a lead article was titled, "Careful Whose Ox You Gore," and that idioms were used by writers throughout the magazine. A casual reading added these to the list:

Throw up their hands
Grinding the axe
Playing the bounce
Get back to the real world
Bit of bouncy
Can opener
Ax to fall
Hat in hand
Cashed strapped
Arm twisting
Whip into shape
Drawn the short straw
Hope springs eternal
On track
Ease off the gas pedal
Lead lining in a golden cloud
Smooth sailing
Add insult to injury
Set the stage
Come on steam
Underwater cemetery

This is a single issue of one magazine.

By turning on the television, we're treated to the same cornucopia of idioms and common phrases. While watching the second game of the 1998 World Series, for instance, we heard, for the first time, the phrase "he went to the kitchen" after a player broke his bat. David Cone, a pitcher for one of the teams, said in an interview that he did not want to be "the weak link" in the team's pitching rotation. That same evening on *Monday Night Football,* Drew Bledsoe, quarterback for the New England Patriots, said that his opponents "had their backs against the wall." On the late-evening news, another famous sports figure was said to have "gotten into a scrape" with the law. And the next morning, while standing in line at a checkout counter, we heard a mother combine two idioms into one sentence to tell her child, "Don't make a scene, you made out like a bandit."

The next evening we "halfheartedly" watched *Law and Order* on TV and heard the following:

Straw man
Barking up the wrong tree
Playing fast and loose
Skip the dance and cut to the song
You're out of your neighborhood
Swirls around the bowl
Get you into the theater but won't let you see the show
Leading a charmed life
Hoity-toity
Pink elephants
Get his shirt dirty
Play Monty Hall
Eye for an eye

Hard sell
Take the fall
First swallows
Busload of nuns
Burning question of the day

Idioms are so popular that many movies have idioms for titles. Checking the weekly *TV Guide,* we found the following movies shown on television:

Diamonds in the Rough
Dog Day Afternoon
Double Take
Dressed to Kill
Far and Away
Fools Rush In
Fun and Fancy Free
Goin' South
Gold Diggers
Head Above Water
In the Blink of an Eye
Loose Cannons
One-Night Stand
Pillow Talk
Point Blank
Promise the Moon
The Rat Race
Shot in the Dark
The Devil's Own
Things Are Tough All Over

To Have and Have Not
Touch and Go
Wing and a Prayer
Scented Souls
Written on the Wind

We take most of our common phrases for granted, not realizing that they are, in fact, idioms and incomprehensible by themselves. Considering how much we speak in idioms, it's a marvel that immigrants or travelers from other lands, armed only with knowledge of literal English, can communicate with us. No wonder both idiom dictionaries and training manuals have been written to help those learning English to identify, understand, and use common phrases in communications.

To try to create a book that would trace the origins of all idioms would be an attempt "to cut a fat hog"—a Texas phrase meaning "to take on more than you can accomplish." (Its origin is obvious.) Those phrases with sketchy or questionable histories, then, we either verified or discarded.

Organizing the phrases for discussion in the chapters to follow presented a problem. We initially thought we would present them according to the period in history in which they were born—an approach that turned out to be too academic. In the end, though, they tended to organize themselves. Since idioms first occur within a narrow context, such as within a war, a trade, or a custom, it seemed only natural to introduce them that way in this book.

We selected for study those phrases that were relatively universal, had an unusual origin, and had historical value. This last aspect, historical value, is especially significant. We learned some fascinating history from tracing the origin of idioms. We hope that you'll appreciate this information as much as we did.

COMMON PHRASES AND
WHERE THEY COME FROM

1
Big Daddies

Long before recorded history began the elders of each generation—particularly those skilled at storytelling—passed along to the children the stories told to them by their forefathers as well as the noteworthy happenings of their own lifetimes. In this fashion the significant historical events and legends of a people were kept alive for future generations, and the cultural heritage was preserved.

From these myths and legends we inherited many common phrases still in use today. Each of the idioms initiated by "a big daddy" of yesteryear could be considered a "blessed event." Yes, this latter idiom typically refers to the birth of a child, but we use it here because the idioms in this chapter enjoyed a legendary birth and a long usage; they are those that originated in ancient mythology.

Crocodile Tears

Why are sham tears or false displays of sorrow called "crocodile tears"?

The story begins in ancient Egypt along the River Nile. One day, out in the wilderness, a group of Egyptians heard what they thought was a person crying. Attracted by the cries, the group went to investigate. They failed to return. The crying began again. A few other Egyptians, more cautious than their former brethren, went to the spot where they heard the crying.

There they were attacked by a monstrous creature. The Egyptians noticed that the reptile moaned and sighed like a human in deep distress. Moreover, the strange creature was the only animal they'd ever encountered that could cover it's eyes with a thin, transparent membrane; when it did so, it created the illusion of blindness. The Egyptians, on their guard, killed the creature. The monster was later named the "crocodile."

With the advance of civilization, crocodiles were discovered to inhabit other lands. Always the experience of the Egyptians was repeated. Eventually humans learned that the crocodile's moans and tears were affected in order to trap victims. Consequently, great precautions were taken to guard against "crocodile tears"—fake sorrow or distress.

Raining Cats and Dogs

It is safe to wager that nobody ever saw cats and dogs fall from the heavens during a rainstorm. Yet whenever there's a heavy downpour, the common phrase we all use is "it's raining cats and dogs." Little do we know that we're taking a page out of ancient northern mythology.

In the myths of the Teutons, an ancient people of either Germanic or Celtic origin who occupied Jutland around

100 B.C., the wind was envisioned as a huge dog that served as chief attendant to Odin, the Norse god of wisdom and war who was responsible for the cosmos. The Teutons believed that when it rained very hard, Odin's dog (in the form of the wind) was chasing a cat (which took the form of the rain). When it poured, then, Odin was dropping "cats and dogs" from the sky.

Science, of course, has dispelled the claims of mythology, but when we're drenched with rain we still revert to the ancient Teutons and mutter, "It's raining cats and dogs."

Gird Up Your Loins

A verbal vestige of Middle Eastern dress from thousands of years ago is the phrase "gird up your loins."

The Semitic tribes of antiquity that roamed and dwelled in the Orient wore loose-fitting robes against the heat of the desert. Whenever they traveled or worked in the fields, they had to tighten or "gird" their robes about their loins. Otherwise their loose-fitting garments would interfere with their freedom of motion.

It was therefore common practice for the early inhabitants of the Orient to wrap their flowing robes around their loins before they went to work—"girding up their loins."

Keep It Sub Rosa

A good way to keep a secret is to caution your confidant to "keep it sub rosa." The Latin lends a dignified touch.

Among the early Teutons the rose was a symbol of secrecy and silence. It was their custom to suspend a rose from the ceilings of their dining rooms—not for the purpose of silencing soup lovers, but to emphasize the strict requirement that nothing said in the house should go beyond its walls. Dining "sub rosa" (under the rose) was a constant reminder to keep secret whatever was said, particularly about absent friends.

Today the high cost of roses prevents us from hanging them from our ceilings, but we continue to keep secrets "sub rosa."

Getting into a Scrape

It's common knowledge that "getting into a scrape" refers to being in a difficult or disagreeable predicament. What's not so universally known is how this expression developed. It can in fact be traced back to the days when England was a huge forest primeval.

To make England inhabitable, its early settlers had to grapple with large herds of wild deer. Well acquainted with the art of hiding when pursued, the deer used their hooves to scrape deep gullies between huge trees and avoid capture. If a settler fell into such a gully, it was difficult to get out. Early English inhabitants knew these gullies as scrapes.

Deer no longer pose a threat, but humans are still "getting into scrapes."

Sixes and Sevens

If the odds are against you or if you are confused or handicapped by a severe hazard, you are at "sixes and sevens."

The regularity with which this phrase recurs in ancient and modern literature is a tribute to the descriptive effects produced by its use.

The phrase originated with the early Mystics, a group that attached great importance to numbers in combination. Thirteen was the unluckiest of all numbers. Add up six and seven and you get thirteen—hence the mystical and unfavorable connotation of "sixes and sevens."

Backgammon enthusiasts have also contributed to the phrase's popularity. In backgammon there are more chances of throwing sixes and sevens than any other numbers. Being at "sixes and sevens" in backgammon is to be playing with the odds against you.

A third variant on this theme relates to sewing needles. When needle sizes were standardized by the first needle manufacturers, sizes six and seven were in greatest demand. This demand caused early factory workers to refer to needles thrown together in confusion with heads and tails mixed up as being at "sixes and sevens."

Deadhead

Through the ages "deadhead" has been a term primarily used by those in the entertainment world to refer to those who gain admission to amusements without paying. More recently it has referred to the legions of devoted Grateful Dead fans who followed the band from city to city, going to dozens of concerts throughout the year.

This phrase dates back to antiquity. Archaeologists have unearthed tiny ivory skulls from the ruins of Pompeii that were used as passes for free admission to the theater. Historians also say that at one time there were so many "deadheads" (the name for Grecian gate crashers) issued that there was practically a "free gate."

Go Whole Hog

"Going whole hog" means "doing whatever you're doing to the limit." John Gower, an English poet in the 1300s, alludes to the phrase's origin in one of his poems:

> But from one piece they thought it hard
> From the whole hog to be disbarred.

The phrase traces its roots back to Muhammad, who, in a sermon to his followers, forbade the eating of one part of a hog—but he forgot to specify which single part of the hog was prohibited. His followers were pious enough, but they were also very hungry. Consequently, to extricate themselves from the dilemma Muhammad had created for them, they cut up a hog into many parts; each person ate a single part. Thus no single worshiper ate "the whole hog," and yet the whole of the hog had been eaten. From this display of practicality came the phrase "go whole hog."

Unaccustomed As I Am to Public Speaking

In the repertoire of most long-winded after-dinner speakers is the phrase "unaccustomed as I am to public speaking." Its modern use is generally insincere. But the man credited as the creator of the phrase was an ancient warrior who had no fear of leading great hosts into battle, but would be dumb-founded if asked to deliver a speech.

According to Ovid, it was the Greek hero Ajax who was the first to say, *"Sed nec mihi dicere prompton,"* which roughly translates into our "unaccustomed as I am to public speaking." When Ajax said it, he was sincere; it was not "clap trap" or "double talk," and no lengthy speech followed.

Leave No Stone Unturned

When the boss wants the job well done, he will tack onto his orders the phrase "leave no stone unturned." By this he means that no effort should be spared in completing the work. This expression has been with us since the days of the Oracle at Delphi in Greek mythology.

You will recall that the Oracle knew the answers to everything, because its source of wisdom was its prophetic communication with the gods. The tale was told by Euripides that one day, when consulted about the whereabouts of a treasure hidden by a vanquished general who had fled, the Oracle counseled that the way to find the treasure was to "leave no stone unturned."

Call a Spade a Spade

When speaking bluntly and to the point without "mincing words," you are "calling a spade a spade." This is another expression that came to us from ancient Greece.

When Lasthenes, as ambassador of Olynthus, called on Philip II of Macedon, he remarked that on his way to the

8

palace he'd heard the Macedonians refer to him (Lasthenes) as a traitor. Philip replied, "Ay, these Macedonians are a blunt people who call figs 'figs' and a spade a 'spade.'" Yet Philip's remark to Lasthenes did not originate with him; he'd borrowed it from Lucian's famous dialogue in which Lucian quoted from Aristophanes, an Athenian playwright most famous for the *Lysistrata*. Aristophanes was the first to give literary form to the ancient Greek saying, "Figs they call figs and a spade a spade."

Lion's Share

If we hear someone say that she paid the "lion's share" of the price of something she bought with others, it means that she paid far more than the other contributors. The phrase not only applies to financial matters but can also denote that an individual has had more than her share of blame, accolade, good fortune, or misfortune. For this phrase we are indebted to Aesop, the ancient Greek who made fables famous.

The phrase "lion's share" comes from the Aesopian tale in which several beasts of the jungle joined the lion in a hunt. When the spoil was to be divided, the lion claimed the first quarter by royal prerogative, he being King of the Beasts. The second quarter he demanded because of his courage, and the third quarter he appropriated for his mate and her cubs. As for the last quarter, he said, "Let who will, dispute it with me." Awed by his prowess, the other beasts yielded and the lion thus obtained his share—the entire booty.

Dog Days of Summer

The Romans called them *canicula res dies,* which translates into "the dog days," or the hottest days of the summer.

According to Roman beliefs, Sirius, the dog star of Roman astrology and the brightest star in the sky for a period of eight weeks (from about July 3 to August 11), rose daily with the sun. Along with the sun Sirius shone brightly throughout "the dog days." So the intense heat during this period was ascribed not only to the heat of the sun but to the intense brightness of the dog star as well.

This ancient use of the term "dog days" for the heat waves of summer, although unscientific, dispels the modern idea that dogs suffer from the heat more readily than do humans—the more common attribution for this phrase.

"Dog" appears often in idioms. Other examples include:

Putting on the dog
Gone to the dogs
Dog and pony show
Dog-eared
Dogface
Dogfight
Dog irons
Dog it
Dog tired
Dog soldier
Doggie bag
In the doghouse
Hangdog
Hot dog

Alpha and Omega of the Matter

Although Greek is no longer a required course of study in most high schools and colleges, there are several phrases taken from the Greek language that we use frequently. "Alpha and omega" is an example.

By "alpha and omega" we mean either "the beginning and the end," or "the core of a discussion." The phrase is analogous to "the A and Z of a matter," for alpha is the first letter of the Greek alphabet and omega is the last.

"Alpha and omega" is used frequently in English literature and also in the speaking vocabulary of preachers and many teachers.

Don't Care a Jot

If you want to express contempt but are eager not to be charged with swearing, you might say, "I don't care a jot." This mild oath has been in use ever since the Hebrew and Greek alphabets have been in existence.

In the ancient Hebrew alphabet the smallest letter is the yod; in the Greek alphabet the smallest is iota. Our English word "jot," meaning "particle," is actually derived from the Hebrew yod and the Greek iota! Both of these letters are written with a mere flourish of the pen, as is their counterpart, the letter I in the Roman alphabet. Thus the ancient Hebrews and early Greeks, by referring to the shortest letters in their alphabets, originated "I don't care a jot."

Cut the Gordian Knot

This phrase refers to an almost impossible feat. But where does it come from? Look no farther than Alexander the Great. He was a man of action who often acted first and thought about it later—a characteristic that gave rise to this common phrase.

When Gordius ruled over Phrygia as the peasant king, he dedicated his chariot to Jupiter and fastened to its beam a yoke with a rope so tightly knotted that no human could untie it by his own hand. Thus, Gordius vowed, "Only he who would untie the knot would rule over Asia." Alexander was determined to rule Asia, however, and consulted the Oracle at Delphi—which concurred with the vow of Gordius. Nevertheless, Oracle or no Oracle, Alexander went to the chariot, uplifted his sword, and "cut the Gordian knot," saying, "'Tis thus Alexander loosens knots." Onward he and his armies went to conquer all Asia.

Go to the Dickens

All lovers of Charles Dickens will be glad to know that he did not inspire the phrase "go to the dickens"—it was popular many centuries before the novelist was born. Instead, credit for this colorful phrase must be given to the early settlers of Scotland.

Like most people of their day, the early Scots believed in evil spirits. In the Scots' case they believed in big devils and little devils. Tiny Satans were known as daikins, and when aroused, an ancient Scot would say, "Go to the daikins." In the course of time "daikins" became "dickens," and from this contraction was born the famous phrase.

Horn of Plenty

This phrase refers to prosperity and abundance. The function of horn-bearing animals' horns is to help them survive: The horns ward off or kill predators, and also help in obtaining food from trees and plants. Yet this "tool" is the symbol of prosperity. Why the contradiction?

For our answer we are once again indebted to Greek mythology. The tale is told that Zeus, the king of the Olympian gods, was born a puny infant. If it had not been for Amalthaea, the goatlike nymph who nursed him, Zeus would have died shortly after birth. Having become fond of Zeus, Amalthaea gave Zeus one of her horns "to remember her by." She said, "Zeus, keep this horn always with thee, for it is endowed with the virtue of becoming filled with whatever its possessor wisheth." Zeus immediately wished that his benefactress be set among the stars, and according to legend Amalthaea still rests there, ever watching Zeus tap plenty from her horn. Thus the horn became the world's symbol for plenty.

Beware of Greeks Bearing Gifts

One of our most popular idiomatic warnings is, "Beware of Greeks bearing gifts"—a caution to be on guard against people who seek to gain our favor by bestowing gifts upon us. Why? It's not the gift itself but rather the motive behind the gift that should concern us.

This phrase dates back to the capture of Troy by the ruse of the famous Trojan horse. If you're not familiar with the story, a gift was made to the besieged city of Troy during the Trojan War—a large wooden horse. When the Trojan residents opened the city doors and wheeled in the horse, they were shocked to discover that in the horse's wooden belly was a Greek army in hiding. This led to the fall of Troy.

No wonder that Virgil said in his *Aeneid, "Timeo danaos et dona ferentes"* (I fear the Danaos and those bearing gifts).

Shout from the Rooftops

Whenever something especially exciting happens to someone and he expresses joyful exuberance, we commonly refer to his behavior as "shouting from the rooftops."

Some trace the origin of this phrase to the old towne crier, an institution brought by our colonial forefathers from England. The crier's duty was to announce the news of the day to citizens assembled in the town commons. Still, the town crier was a modern and newfangled public address system compared with his predecessor, the housetop crier of ancient Middle Eastern cities.

The Syrians are credited with having the first town criers. The houses in their cities were made with flat roofs, and when the heat became excessive they often slept on the housetops. Here, too, they assembled to gossip and celebrate their festivities.

So after a particularly hot evening, with throngs assembled on their roof, it was the duty of the town crier to await the arrival of the sun from the top of his house every morning and "shout" its arrival "from the rooftops," along with the news and orders of the day.

Lily or White Livered

Someone cowardly and weak is often referred to as "lily livered." In ancient days the liver, not the heart, was considered the place where amorous affections were located, and a man's love was only as good as his liver.

It was said that the "liver of a coward contained no blood." His arteries and veins were white, as white as a lily. Such a man was called "white" or "lily livered" and was held in contempt by the fair sex.

Both the Greeks and the Romans attached great significance to the liver in a religious rite known as the Auspices that was held before important events, particularly battles, to foretell their outcome. At this ritual, animals were sacrificed. If the livers of the sacrificial animals were healthy and red blooded, the omen was favorable; but if the livers were pale, defeat or hardship was forecast.

By Heck

By far the mildest oath and the least likely to cause discomfort in mixed company is "by heck." After universal usage for centuries, it has become free from the stigma of "cussing."

"By heck" has a very heroic origin. It derives from the Greek exclamation "by Hector," which named one of the sons of Achilles. Patroclus, with the help of Athena, took Hector for a chariot ride around the ancient city of Troy. Unfortunately for Hector, he was not in the chariot but tied behind it and dragged into Achilles's camp mutilated and dead, all because Hector had caused trouble by slaying too many men. Over time "by Hector" was shortened to "by heck."

There are some who prefer a different version of its origin: Hecate, the Greek goddess of the underworld, made her legions of underlings swear an oath to her. Originally "by Hecate," the oath was later abbreviated to its present form.

The common experiences of romance, courtship, marriage, and raising a family have all given rise to frequently used phrases. Those listed in this chapter were born from mythology.

As Handsome as Adonis

So frequently do we refer to men of enviable physical build and perfectly formed features as being "handsome as Adonis" that some believe there is among us now a modern-day man whose name is Adonis. Alas, no such person exists; the Adonis to whom our phrase refers was, is, and always will be a myth.

Again we are indebted to Greek mythology. When the Greek gods and goddesses ruled the universe, Adonis was a young Greek hunter possessed of perfect physical form. Because he was too handsome for this cruel earth, he was killed by a wild boar.

Aphrodite, the goddess of love, did not want to give Adonis to Persephone, the queen of Hades. The two goddesses thus called upon Zeus, the king of all the deities, to arbitrate their claims. In his great wisdom, almighty Zeus decreed: "Adonis should spend one-third of each year with Aphrodite, one-third with Persephone, and one-third by himself."

During the one-third of a year when Adonis was alone, he was so overcome thinking about Aphrodite's and Persephone's attentions that he coined the phrase "handsome as Adonis."

Apple of My Eye

It was believed as long ago as the ninth century that the pupil of the eye was a vital spot in the human anatomy. Primitive medical curiosity about it caused the early healers to study the pupil as closely as they could. They concluded that it was apple shaped, and so it became popularly known as "the apple of the eye." Because the pupil was considered as vital as life itself, it became customary for a gallant hero to call the object of his affections "the apple of my eye."

Honeymoon

The first recorded data concerning the phenomenon of the "honeymoon" is found among the early writings of the

Northern European countries. Newly married couples were required—actually compelled—to drink, from one full moon to the next full moon (about thirty days), a wine derived from fermented honey and water and called metheglin. It was believed that a thirty-day diet of metheglin furnished newlyweds with sufficient sweetness to carry out their marriage vows in perpetuity. Some of the newlyweds took their metheglin intake so seriously that they perished from it. That was the fate of Attila, the great warrior, who imbibed so much honey at his wedding feast that he drank himself to death.

Marriage Knot

Among the ancients knots had more than symbolic significance, and originally the "marriage knot" was as literal as it was figurative. There are several possible origins for this common phrase.

The early Hindu marriage ceremony included a literal tying of a knot by the bridegroom. At the ceremony's end he would put a brightly colored ribbon around his bride's neck. Before the knot was tied, the bride's father could refuse consent and demand a better price for his daughter. But once the groom tied the ribbon his father-in-law could make no further demands; the bride became the groom's forever, for among the Hindus marriage was indissoluble.

At the nuptials of a Parsee couple (this Zoroastrian religious sect in India descended from the Persians), it was the *groom* who was knotted . . . with a sevenfold cord! The cord was made of seven strands not only to keep the groom wellbound but also because, among the Parsees, seven was both a sacred and a lucky number.

In Carthage the bride and the groom were tied to each other with leather laces bound around the thumbs of the contracting parties.

At a Roman wedding service the groom was required to loosen the knot of his beloved's girdle. So tight was this knot that the Romans called it *nodus hercules,* the "Herculean knot," for Herculean strength was required to untie it.

Better Half

A plaintive, tear-jerking tale out of the ancient Middle East is the origin of the modern spouse's humility when introducing his mate as his "better half."

The story tells of a Bedouin who had offended his prince. The Bedouin's wife pleaded for her spouse's life:

"O great Prince, the blasphemy is horrible, I confess.

But it is not my whole husband who has thus rendered himself guilty toward Thee."

"Not thy whole husband," the Prince replied.

"Nay," she continued, "it is but half, the half of him that has committed the insult; for am I not the other half, I who have never offended Thee? Now the guilty half places itself under the protection of the innocent half and the latter cannot suffer the former to be punished."

From this ancient concept of a man and woman being merged into one by marriage comes our phrase "better half."

Best Man

The chief function of the best man at a wedding has not always been serving as keeper of the ring. When knights wore armor and chivalry reigned, best men were required to do considerably more.

In feudal days a rival of the groom, if he was any kind of a gallant, took an oath to carry off the bride before or during the nuptials. Since marriages were arranged and the groom often wasn't the bride's first choice, romantic triangles were not uncommon. In order to avoid the rival, most nuptials took place under cover of night. Fortunate was the groom who could get as a best man a worthy and versatile warrior to defend him against his rival should he discover where and when the wedding was to take place.

A wise best man would enlist a coterie of ushers in armor who were expert lancers to accompany him to the ceremony. Behind the altars of many a feudal church were stored for emergency use by wedding parties huge collections of long lances with torch sockets. The lances were used both for defense and for illumination during a getaway. Only the bravest of the brave volunteered to attend a bridegroom at his nuptials, and the best man was truly the best man, for if he was unable to fight down the groom's rival and his supporters, the groom would lose his bride.

2
Scrapes

The common phrases discussed in this chapter all arose from the conditions of warfare, even though the first five are ostensibly about marriage! Nevertheless, we all know that conflict and even "war" can exist in courtship and marriage.

Even Steven

" 'Now we are even,' quoth Steven, when he gave his wife six blows to one!"

This quote from Jonathan Swift's *Letters to Stella* is responsible for the phrase "even Steven." When *Letters to Stella* was first published, the six-blows-to-one conception of equality was not as disproportionate as it sounds today. In Swift's time equal rights for women were unknown. With the advent of women's suffrage and social legislation for women, however, the modern ratio is approaching one to one and hence evolved into "even Steven," which today is synonymous with "tit for tat" or "in balance." "Even Steven" acquired its first extensive use in America immedi-

ately after the Civil War, when, for Reconstruction purposes, Confederate currency was taken in exchange for federal.

Even more recently, in the popular television situation
comedy *Seinfeld* an episode involved Jerry realizing that
his whole life could be characterized by the phrase "even
Steven": No matter what happened to him, he always came
out even in the end.

Rule of Thumb

When we use established past practices as a guideline for making a decision, we often refer to "rules of thumb."

In 1732 Francis Buller, an English judge, proclaimed
that a "man could not beat his wife with a stick larger than
the diameter of his thumb." Regardless of Buller's inten-
tion, his "rule of thumb" was taken seriously by many, resulting in a large public outcry accompanied by satirical
cartoons. The remark was never forgotten, as it was attributed to him in biographies written after his death.

While Buller is credited with the phrase's origin, in reality it was probably used much earlier: The "thumb" was a
unit of measurement in the late seventeenth century.

Mad Money

Sometimes we hear a woman say that she is going shopping
and is taking her "mad money." By this she means that the
shopping spree is unplanned; she doesn't really need anything, but she's going to buy it anyway.

At the turn of the twentieth century American women began to go on dates without chaperones. Consequently, the wise woman took some money with her in case her date made unwanted sexual advances and she needed to leave him and get herself home. Because the woman would undoubtedly be furious at her date for placing her in such a predicament, her emergency fund was called "mad money."

Making Ends Meet

"Making ends meet" is often associated with an inability to stay afloat financially. Who would have thought that a phrase that now applies to the continual economic struggles of common folks would have evolved from the ordeal connected with obtaining the funds necessary to dress a well-heeled lady properly?

To be dressed properly, the lady of fashion of the eighteenth and nineteenth centuries often required assistance in pulling together the two ends of her corset, and then buckling it when both ends met. Her dress would not hang properly unless a helper, generally her maligned husband, had hooked together numerous latchets and hooks and eyes, all of which required tedious and cautious pulling to "make the ends meet." Even a lady's shoes and galoshes of yesteryear were equipped with leather thongs, the ends of which had to be brought together before they could be buckled. From all this strenuous effort of pulling corsets, dresses, and shoes together came the phrase "making ends meet."

At first the expression referred simply to the physical ordeal accompanying a lady's getting dressed up. As the cost of her ensemble increased and the difficulty in putting it together diminished, "making ends meet" came to refer to the financial ordeal connected with gathering the funds necessary to dress a lady properly.

Pin Money

"Pin money," in the minds of most wives—but not necessarily in those of their husbands—is money set aside to meet their needs and wants.

It's hard to imagine a day and age when pins were items of considerable value and were sold just two days of the year, January 1 and 2. But such was the state of affairs in the early twentieth century, when pins were first introduced in the market. At that time they commanded a hefty price. The money a husband gave his wife for the purchase of pins was sizable enough to be given the name "pin money."

So much "hullabaloo" was caused by the first pins produced in England that a wife often inserted in her marriage contract a special clause giving her a lien on the rents collected from her husband's land. This clause was named the Pin-Money Charge and was enforced by the courts as a valid contractual marital right.

As the production of pins became more commonplace, their value decreased. But not so the sums claimed by wives for "pin money." The phrase now embraces every variety of feminine wants and desires.

The following phrases emerged from preparations for battle, the "war room," the journey to battle, the battlefield itself, the moments following a battle, or an army's occupation of a defeated country. Others were evolved by pirates who—either with the blessing of a particular government or as "freelancers"—were engaged in one form of sea terror or another.

Don't Kick a Man When He's Down

One of the first rules of good sportsmanship is never to take advantage of an opponent when he is helpless and unable to fight back. This rule is based upon the old maxim "don't kick a man when he's down," coined around A.D. 555 by Belisarius, a discredited Roman general under Emperor Justinian.

Belisarius had been Justinian's commander of the Roman forces in the East. Justinian accused him of conspiring against him and, as a consequence, stripped Belisarius of his command, his rank, and his wealth. Belisarius later became blind and turned to begging at the gates of Rome for his livelihood. Passersby were likely to kick beggars, and whenever Belisarius was kicked he would remind the assailant of his former high station by crying, "Don't kick a man when he's down." Such wisdom was seldom heard from beggars, and would often lead to an inquiry about Belisarius's identity. When told of his former high rank in the Roman army, a passerby was more likely to make a substantial donation. Other beggars, noticing Belisarius's success, picked up the chant, and thus it traveled until it became the rallying cry of the downtrodden throughout the world.

Stick to Your Last

Around 350 B.C. there lived in Greece a very famous painter named Apelles. It was his practice to conceal himself at previews of his paintings in order to hear the public's opinions of his masterpieces. If he heard any criticism that he believed would improve his work, he made use of it.

At one such preview a cobbler criticized the shoes in a painting on which Apelles had labored long and hard. After altering the picture to cure the defect noted by the cobbler, the painter arranged a second preview. This time the bootmaker began to criticize the anatomy of one of the characters. Apelles, knowing that the criticism was unjust and that the cobbler knew nothing about anatomy, was unable to restrain himself. From his hiding place he shouted, "Cobbler, stick to your last!"

From that time it has been the custom to debunk dilettantes and all others who purport to know what they do not with the pointed caution, "Stick to your last."

A Pyrrhic Victory

When the cost of success is greater than its reward, we say we have won "a Pyrrhic victory."

This phrase was inspired originally by Pyrrhus, king of Epirus, a kingdom in the northwestern part of ancient

Greece, after an early victory over the Romans at the battle of Asculum in 279 B.C. In the battle Pyrrhus lost the flower of his army. When his few surviving lieutenants offered Pyrrhus their congratulations, he said to them, "One more such victory over the Romans and we are utterly undone." The fears of Pyrrhus proved true. After his victory at Asculum, Pyrrhus was defeated by the Romans under Manius Curius Dentatus in 276 B.C.

The battle of Asculum was a barren victory. Historians referred to it as "a Pyrrhic victory" with such regularity that the phrase has now come to refer to a victory in name but a defeat in fact.

Scrape Up an Acquaintance

To "scrape up an acquaintance" is to get to know someone hitherto unknown to us.

Among the long line of Roman emperors was a man named Hadrian, who ruled from A.D. 117 to 132. He was famous both as a warrior and as an emperor, and it was his practice to inspect the Roman public baths. During one tour of inspection he saw an old soldier who was well known to him scraping himself with a piece of broken pottery called, in those days, a potsherd. These were used by the poor instead of a brush. Hadrian felt that the venerable veteran merited a brush, so he gave the man money with which to purchase one. Visiting the public baths again on the following day, Hadrian observed that practically every bather was using a clay potsherd instead of a brush. Realizing he had started something, Hadrian said, "Scrape on, gentlemen, but you will not scrape up an acquaintance with me." And thus Emperor Hadrian gave the world a new idiom.

Cross the Rubicon

An irrevocable act of important consequence is commonly called "crossing the Rubicon."

The Rubicon is a small river that in the days of Julius Caesar separated Italy from Cisalpine Gaul, and it played an important part in Caesar's military career. Through most of Caesar's life Gaul was as far as his territory extended, but he longed to extend his empire farther into Italy.

After considerable hesitation, Caesar decided to cross the Rubicon in force, realizing that by so doing he could never retrace his steps: If civil war ensued, it would destroy his power forever. Fortunately, things went Caesar's way. Crossing the Rubicon allowed Caesar to start full blast on the campaigns that ultimately made him the "Great Caesar."

Since then it has been customary to refer to undertaking critical and irrevocable acts as "crossing the Rubicon."

Roman Holiday

Whenever someone is sacrificed to amuse the general public, the spectacle is called a "Roman holiday." Historically it would be more accurate to call it an "Etruscan holiday."

Before the rise of Rome, the region of Italy between the Arno and Tiber Rivers and extending inland to the Apennine Mountains was called the nation of Etruria; its citizens were known as Etruscans. When Etruria was conquered by the Romans, the Etruscan civilization was transplanted to Rome. One of the Etruscan practices adopted by the Romans was the custom of honoring dead war heroes by sacrificing the lives of captives seized in battle. These human sacrifices were gala events among the Etruscans, but they weren't exciting enough for the insatiable Romans, who converted them into public gladiatorial contests in which the captives killed each other while the Roman citizens beheld the gory spectacle.

The gladiatorial combats were so relished by the Romans that the days set apart for them were declared "Roman holidays." Hence their name in history and our own interpretation of them: a crushing defeat of a distinguished foe, generally inflicted before a vast audience.

Throw Dust in the Eyes

The expression "throwing dust in the eyes" means "intentionally deceiving or causing confusion."

When the Greeks and Romans were the military leaders of the world, they conducted their battles with crude equipment. The closest they could come to a modern-day blitzkrieg was to stir up and throw sufficient dust into the air to blind their enemies and create mass confusion.

Much later Muhammad, a warrior of note as well as a religious leader, employed a "dust-krieg" in the battle of Honein. The following reference is made to it in the Koran:

"Neither didst thou Muhammad cast dust into their eyes; but it was God who confounded them."

On another occasion the Moreishites surrounded Muhammad's house, bent upon slaying him. They peered through his door and saw him asleep. Just then Muhammad's son-in-law, Ali, came out of nowhere and threw into the air great handfuls of dust. He failed to throw enough dust to save himself, but Muhammad escaped because of Ali's "dust-krieg" upon his attackers. Thus from this ancient military technique we derived our common phrase "throwing dust in the eyes."

The Die Is Cast

Whenever we say, "The die is cast," we attach finality and resolution to the job at hand; there is no turning back.

Julius Caesar was a man of his word; he never took back anything he said. His soldiers knew this well. They may have experienced some apprehension about his plans before he took them across the Rubicon, but once they set foot on the opposite bank and he made his historic utterance, "The dice have been thrown," they knew there would be no turning back.

To this day the import of Caesar's words is clear in our use of "the die is cast" to attach finality to a situation. Because many of us are less ambitious than Caesar, we use the singular form.

Buckle Down to Work

At the turn of the year, when it is seasonable to make firm resolutions for the New Year, many of us resolve to "Buckle down to work." This phrase means to do a job seriously and well; it also can imply a heroic effort. Little do we realize, when we make this resolve, that we have borrowed a phrase from the days of knighthood.

When a knight had a serious battle to fight, his first task was to summon his gentleman's gentleman, who took out the knight's suit of armor, gave it a thorough oiling, and then proceeded to the business of actually "buckling" the armor onto his master's body. This task was a crucial preliminary to the combat ahead, and unless it was executed carefully the knight would not live to fight another battle. So the "work" buckled down to was actually a matter of life and death.

Bloodbath

Two horribly bloody events that took place in the sixteenth century are sources of our modern expression "bloodbath."

One is the massacre of the Huguenots at Vessy, France, in 1562; the other is the wholesale murder in 1520 of seventy Swedish nobles of Stockholm. Christian II of Denmark commanded the brutal executions of the noblemen—executions so ruthless that a literal bath of human blood formed.

The Huguenot massacre, the foul brainstorm of the duke of Guise, was also merciless in its horrors. Both of these displays of bloody brutality so vividly affected the masses that when they spoke of them they referred to each as a "bloodbath."

To the Last Ditch

An act of courage today is often referred to as "a stand to the last ditch."

It was William, prince of Orange (later King William III of England), who first uttered this symbolic phrase. In 1672, shortly after William of Orange was established as stadholder of the United Netherlands, both England and France were at war with the Netherlands. When his cause appeared lost, the duke of Buckingham asked William whether he did not see defeat looming before his country. William answered, "Nay, there is one certain means by which I can be sure never to see my country's defeat. I will die in the last ditch."

He rejected all peace offers, opened the sluices of the Netherlands' dikes, flooded large areas of land, checked the threatened invasion, drove his foes into Holland, and climaxed his efforts with treaties with England and France, giving him ultimate victory. "To the last ditch" became the motto of William's troops, and for us it has come to denote the firm resolve to see a thing through no matter how great the obstacles.

Feather in Your Cap

When a person has solved a difficult problem or earned an honor that will help her obtain a future goal—perhaps a job promotion or a better assignment—we say that she has earned a "feather in her cap." Nowadays, of course, feathers typically adorn women's headwear, but it was not always so. Originally the feather was the prerogative of males, and only of the brave and strong.

Among the warriors of tribal days, it was the practice of the chief of a tribe to reward his stalwarts with a feather for each killed foe a fighter could produce. This custom persisted among civilized nations. When wars became less frequent, the expression "a feather in your cap" became symbolic of an earned honor.

History records that the Lycians, an ancient people in Asia Minor, awarded feathers to their warriors for bravery. In early Hungary, it was expressly prescribed by law that "none might wear a feather but he who has slain a Turk." The Chinese, a people of carefully preserved custom and procedure, attached great significance to the wearing of the feather of a peacock. At first only the Chinese who had performed valorously for their fatherland could wear such plumage. Later they would occasionally so honor a foreigner. For example, in 1864 a Chinese emperor declared General Charles George Gordon (commonly known as Chinese Gordon or Gordon Pasha) a mandarin of the first class for his success in leading an irregular army of peasants and adventurers to quell the Taiping Rebellion against the Manchu Dynasty. The formal ceremony accompanying this naming included the bestowal of a royal feather and a yellow jacket.

Ladies began to wear feathers in their hats after one romantic warrior, in an amorous moment, gave his beloved his hard-earned feather as a token of his troth.

Hard Lines

"Hard lines," a frequently used phrase, means "bad luck."

Before the advent of modern warfare, the lines of soldiers used for front and firing duties suffered the most casualties. Soldiers, therefore, called an assignment to the front firing lines a call to the "hard lines"—the position where they were most apt to experience the severest hardships and dangers.

From the military, soldiers carried "hard lines" to civilian life. Now the phrase is used by anybody to denote any kind of difficulty or trouble.

Turncoat

An opportunist whose loyalty is determined by whoever is in power is a "turncoat."

The term was first applied to the duke of Saxony, whose allegiances during the Thirty Years' War changed so often that the following fable is told. The duke's land, situated between French and Spanish possessions, served as a battleground in the war raging between the two countries. The duke owned a reversible coat. When the battle was going well for Spain, he showed Spain's color of blue. When France was winning, he reversed the coat and wore the French white. When his antics were discovered, the soldiers berated him with the scornful howl, "Behold the turncoat."

From the duke of Saxony's reversible coat came our term for people who try to play all ends against the middle.

Between the Devil and the Deep Blue Sea

When someone is in a situation from which he cannot save himself, we say that he's "between the devil and the deep blue sea."

It was one Colonel Munro who coined this phrase while serving for Sweden against Austria in the Thirty Years' War. At one point in the advance Colonel Munro, because the Swedes had not given their cannon sufficient elevation, found his troops moving toward the Austrians in the direct line of fire of their own battery divisions to the rear. He quickly dispatched a messenger to the commanding Swedish battery officer with the note: "Raise your cannons, we are between the devil and the deep blue sea." The cannons were raised, and the battle was won. Ever since, "between the devil and the deep blue sea" has been a handy phrase used by people of all climes when caught on the horns of a dilemma.

Don't Give a Damn

Sayings come and go, but "don't give a damn" keeps rolling along. Unlike many emphatic terms, it is not a vulgarism. *Damn* is a dictionary word with several meanings.

When used emphatically, it alludes to an old Hindu coin that was used extensively in India, the value of which fluctuated greatly throughout the centuries. It reached a high of one-fortieth of a rupee and a low of a one-thousandth of a rupee. When the damn was at its lowest, British troopers, because they could get little for it, used its name to describe valueless things or facts. The saying, because of its succinctness, has become the leader of forceful speech wherever English is spoken.

Run the Gauntlet

When someone is criticized from all sides, he is said to have "run the gauntlet."

This is a figurative version of a military practice used by the English army many centuries ago to punish soldiers who had violated orders. The commanding officer would form his company into two lines of men armed with switches and staves. The culprit would be ordered to strip to the waist and run between the two lines while his fellow company members hit him with their switches or staves. The runway between the two lines was called the "gantlet," resulting in the original version of this phrase.

Later, when gloves became part of military dress, the practice of using switches was dropped and the paddling was done with gloves. Originally the gloves were called "gauntlets," and hence the practice was called "running the gauntlet."

Catch a Tarter

"To catch a Tarter," like "to bite off more than you can chew," means to tackle more than you can handle.

During a battle an Irish fighter for England would capture a ferocious Tarter, but the Tarter would many times refuse to return to the camp of the Irishman; nor would he allow the Irishman to return alone. Until help arrived, the

Irishman was stymied. This experience became a classic story among the Expeditionary Forces, and from it developed the saying "catch a Tarter."

Blarney

Suave talk, cajolery, beguiling speech, or bewitching romancing are a few of the descriptive categories covered by "blarney."

In 1862 there lived a mighty Irish patriot who was suave of speech and most resourceful of wit. His name was Cormack McCarthy. McCarthy and some of his compatriots did a little revolting against the king of England, and they were finally surrounded in a castle in the village of Blarney, not far from Cork. McCarthy negotiated an armistice with his captors, agreeing to surrender Blarney Castle within a few days. But instead of doing so, he sent out to the English evasive messages full of weaselly "clap trap." Finally, Lord Carew, commander of the British army, suspected that shrewd McCarthy was merely "whiling away time" pending the arrival of additional rebels, and he admitted that he'd been duped by the man. He then yelled to McCarthy, "That's the Blarney" and stormed the castle.

In one of the walls of Blarney Castle lies a stone that's difficult to touch because it overhangs a moat. Around this stone has developed a myth that whoever succeeds in kissing it becomes endowed with both suavity and the ability to lie with a straight face. Many modern tourists, when near Cork, go out to Blarney Castle to kiss the "Blarney Stone."

The Coast Is Clear

"The coast is clear" means that the way is safe or you can proceed without worry.

The saying held a place of honor in all pirate handbooks. It was the cry raised on every pirate ship when land was sighted. After the captain had been advised by his lookout, who verified with his telescope that no one was on shore to witness their secret landing, he would shout, "The coast is clear." Now that sea piracy has been relegated to the legendary past, "the coast is clear" has been put to more responsible uses—though it can still aid those who commit mischief.

Walk the Plank

In the working world to "walk the plank" is to be forced out of a job (that is, get fired).

When piracy was rampant, it was the custom of the sea for pirates to dispose of their captives by tying them up and forcing them to walk along a plank laid across the bulwark of a ship until they overbalanced and fell into the sea. There they met death by drowning.

Armed to the Teeth

Also out of pirate lore comes the phrase "armed to the teeth," which means to be so perfectly fortified that nothing more can be added.

When pirates were on duty, they had guns in both hands, daggers and loaded guns in all their pockets (guns in those days were capable of carrying only one shot, so instead of reloading, shooters carried many guns on their person) knives in their headwear, and, appropriately, a knife between their teeth, the last place a capable pirate could carry a weapon.

Devil's Own

When you want to describe the antics of a very spirited and dashingly daring individual, you say, "She's the devil's own."

The author of this expression was General Picton, commander of the famous Eighty-Eighth Foot Regiment of the British forces in the Peninsular War (1809–14). The regiment was composed of men from Connaught who were known as the "Connaught Boys."

It was the daring and devil-may-care spirit of the Eighty-Eighth that brought victory to the English. When asked to describe the fighting spirit of his men, Picton said, "They are the devil's own." The phrase struck the fancy of the English, and it has been used ever since to denote spirited and dashing human conduct.

Give No Quarter

To extend no mercy to an opponent is to "give no quarter."

When the Spaniards and Dutch decided in 1629 to end the wars they had waged against each other during the Thirty Years' War, they signed a treaty of peace that provided for the manner of disposition and release of prisoners. It was agreed mutually that all officers and soldiers who were prisoners should be ransomed by their government for one-quarter of their pay. This manner of release of prisoners proved popular with the masses. Consequently, they coined from it two phrases: "To give no quarter" meant "to be merciless," and "to give quarter" referred to an extension of mercy.

Bury the Hatchet

The old saying "bury the hatchet" refers to making peace with someone with you've quarreled with. This custom came from Native Americans.

The Native Americans had a quaint way of letting "bygones be bygones." When an armistice was declared between two warring parties, no one could attend the peace meeting until all the warriors had actually buried their hatchets (tomahawks). Bows and arrows were retained just in case, but before the Calumet (the pipe of peace) could be puffed the tomahawks had to be under the sod. If the peace negotiations went awry, the tomahawks were disinterred. No good Native American ever forgot where he buried his hatchet.

Face the Music

The phrase "face the music" refers to coming to grips with an unpleasant situation—often a case in which we must confront someone we have wronged.

In the days when wars were fought exclusively on land, whenever the troops were about to go into battle the band was at the head of the line. They played martial airs while the lines were forming. The command immediately preceding the "forward march" order was "face the music." Every soldier knew its meaning.

Another possible origin of the phrase is the process of drumming a soldier out of service. With the entire company at attention, drums are rolled to the tune of the "Rogue's March."

Among theatrical performers "face the music" refers to the courage an actor must have to gaze at the playing musicians in the orchestra pit with the spotlight turned right on him.

All Hang Together

When a group undertakes a project, all group members know that they share equally the blame or the criticism for the result; they say, "We must all hang together." So commonplace is our use of this jargon that we forget its original reference: to the gloomy prospect of death by hanging.

The originator of this phrase was John Hancock, the first signer of the Declaration of Independence. When Hancock penned his name to that noble document, he said, "We must all hang together; else we shall all hang separately." The spectrum of hanging was ever present in the minds of our revolutionary ancestors. On a visit home, Washington's mother greeted him with, "Well, I see that they have not hanged you yet."

Flash in the Pan
and
Lock, Stock, and Barrel

The colonial rifle gave rise to these two phrases. A spurt of activity that quickly passes into oblivion is known to Americans as "a flash in the pan." Athletes who rise to stardom quickly and then vanish just as quickly from the scene are described as "flashes in the pan." Collectors of early American firearms may be familiar with the roots of this phrase.

The antiquated flintlock gun, in addition to its barrel, had a pan that contained the priming powder. If a spark from the flintlock ignited the priming power fully, the main charge would go off as expected. But if there was only "a flash in the pan"—that is, a smoldering fire—the main charge would not go off.

The principal parts of the flintlock gun were its lock, its stock, and its barrel. Because of the importance of the gun in colonial times, the phrase "lock, stock, and barrel" began to denote the whole of anything important.

Bag and Baggage

To be off on your way hurriedly and unceremoniously, leaving behind no property whatsoever, comprises the sense of "to go bag and baggage." In the case of an unwelcome guest, the host whose privacy has been invaded likely wishes the guest would depart "bag and baggage."

In warfare the "dog soldiers" who are most "on the ball" (who move the fastest) are, "on balance," the victors. For this reason, everything an army does, it does speedily. The soldier's kit, originally called the soldier's bag, contains only what is absolutely necessary. The army's baggage is portable and easily assembled and disassembled—it is always "on ice," or in a state of constant readiness. In army circles, "moving bag and baggage" refers to the preliminary work connected with moving the army from one location to another and "setting up shop." It is characterized by being "on a roll," or excitement and feverish activity when completing an important task.

Because there is generally considerable flurry when people embark upon a journey, it was only natural to borrow a term from the military and apply it to the excited movement of civilian travelers.

Tell It to the Marines

Nowadays if you tell a young person something she doesn't believe, you may hear, "Gimme a break," or "Yeah, right." But someone a bit older might respond, "Tell it to the marines."

With the growth of the British Empire, it became necessary to confine the activities of the Royal Navy to the manning of vessels and the patrolling of the seas; a separate force of men, the Royal Marines, was organized to police the various British possessions. The first recruits to the marines knew nothing of navigation or seamanship. While being transported to their land service stations by the Royal Navy, they were the butt of many practical jokes perpetrated upon them by the regular sailors. The gullible young marines were told many a fanciful and imaginary tale of experiences at sea. As a result, the first marines were called "gulpins"—which, to a sailor, means a person who believes anything he's told. Before long, if one sailor told his mate an incredible story, the mate would reply, "Tell it to the marines."

To Be Knocked into a Cocked Hat

To be routed utterly in a physical or verbal contest is "to be knocked into a cocked hat."

This expression came into use when it was the practice of military officers to wear soft hats, which, by habit, they flattened out and carried under their arms. Hats crushed this way became triangular shaped when completely flattened. The thought behind "knocked into a cocked hat" is that when someone was routed, he was flattened out as completely as an officer's cocked hat.

The phrase has taken on additional meaning in the game of bowling. "To be knocked into a cocked hat" has come to refer to the difficult situation a player finds herself in when only the kingpin and the two end pins are left standing. When this happens, the three remaining pins form a triangle similar to the officer's cocked hat. The player is flattened, because to strike down pins so arranged is very difficult.

3
Toothbrush Day

 Through the ages humans have dealt with those who violated the rules of larger society. Yet historically, views of appropriate justice have "backed and filled," or vacillated, between punishment and rehabilitation accompanied by restitution—as they still do today.

From this "legal smorgasbord," many idioms arose. Most of the common phrases we have selected for inclusion in this chapter originated during a period when "thin gruel" and fear of such punishment abounded. To illustrate the severity of the punishments inflicted, "gruel" is, by definition, a "thin watery soup." So "thin gruel," an idiom denoting severe punishment, emphasizes how badly prisoners were fed and cared for.

In court judges "threw the book" at most suspects, and punishment was meted out "in cold blood," leaving suspects no choice but to "bite the bullet"—if not "bite the dust."

By the way, those who are curious about the chapter's title will find that this idiom refers to the day of a court appearance. On this day the defendant is told to bring along a toothbrush because, more than likely, he would end up "in the jug." This idiom itself arose from the old Scottish iron yoke, called a jough (pronounced *jugs*), in which criminals were held before the advent of jails. The idiom was later applied to jails, considered at the time nothing more than large "jugs."

Gone to the Dogs

A person who has wasted his life, or money that has been spent foolishly, is said to have "gone to the dogs." This phrase is of Chinese origin and is as ancient as its place of birth.

In the Far East, thousands of years ago, dogs were not permitted within the walls of a city. Forbidden also was the disposal of refuse within the city limits. Consequently, all refuse was taken beyond the city walls to a large dumping ground. Here stray dogs would gather and search for food amid the refuse. The trash was then said to have "gone to the dogs."

When the practice developed of expelling criminals and other undesirables from within the city walls, those so banished were also said to have "gone to the dogs," because their fate was similar to that of the refuse—they were often attacked and eaten by the hungry dogs.

Won't Hold Water

If an argument is flawed or an item has a defect, we say, "It won't hold water." This phrase has its roots in Roman mythology.

Tutia was one of the original Vestal Virgins—the women who tended the fire in Rome's Temple of Vesta and who were required to remain virgins during their office. Tutia was suspected of having lost her claim to that distinction and was asked by the Pontifex Maximus to prove her innocence.

The method of proof was ingenious. Tutia was required to carry a sieve full of water from the Tiber River to the Temple of Vesta. If the sieve held the water she was innocent; if it did not she was guilty. The punishment for failure was to be buried alive. Tutia passed the test. But ever since, the phrase "it won't hold water" has been used to describe anything that cannot pass the test for integrity or soundness.

Go Through Fire and Water

There are some human experiences so full of wretchedness, pain, and suffering that they have all the "earmarks" of trying ordeals. It is natural, then, to refer to the ancient trials by the ordeals of fire and water in our phrase "go through fire and water." This phrase is most certainly a relic of English history that preceded our modern trials by juries, when all trials were "by ordeal." Two more common phrases, "in hot water" and "over the coals" were preceded by the less frequently used "to go through fire and water."

Which ordeal a prisoner had to survive to prove his innocence depended upon the nature of the crime with which he was charged. The most common ordeals were those of fire and water. If a defendant's lot was fire he had to walk barefooted over a bed of live coals. If he came through the ordeal of fire without burning his feet, he was innocent. If his ordeal was water and he failed to drown when immersed he was acquitted.

The horrors of the old ordeals of fire and water were so intense that whenever one endured an unpleasant experience it was said that he or she had to go "through fire and water." Trial by jury has supplanted the ordeals of fire and water, but the phrase "go through fire and water" keeps rolling along.

In Hot Water

The phrase "to be in hot water" is defined as being in an intensely unpleasant situation, but its meaning is never literal. Such was not the case hundreds of years ago.

In feudal days, there were no courts of law and no trials by jury. Instead, one was dealt "ordeal justice" and "trials by ordeal." The form of the ordeal depended upon the nature of the crime. If it carried the death penalty, the ordeal was by either fire or hot water. And if hot water was ordered, the accused would be put into a huge cauldron of boiling water. If the accused survived the ordeal, an acquittal followed. If scalded to death, the accused was considered to have been guilty.

So in feudal days to be "in hot water" was to be charged with a capital crime. Today justice is meted out more humanely, but the saying is still used to describe uncomfortable or dangerous situations.

Hauled Over the Coals

At one time coals served the same purpose as the modern courtroom. From this practice we inherited the popular catchphrase "to be hauled over the coals," a saying employed when we are called to account for some shortcoming or misdeed.

At the feudal "ordeal of fire," live coals were the juries. A defendant was required to walk over a large bed of glowing coals. Kings used this strategy most effectively to force money lenders not only to reduce their interest rates but also to "remember" that an old loan had been paid.

As late as the time written about in *Ivanhoe,* "hauling over the coals" was a frequent practice. Sir Walter Scott referred to it in his novel when Front de Boeuf threatened Isaac with a "hauling over the coals."

Go to Pot

Forget that marijuana is called "pot" and that habitual smokers of the drug are called "potheads." The origin of "go to pot" has nothing to do with either. There are two versions of the source of this common phrase—which means "to deteriorate or lose control of your moral restraints, fortitude, or will."

The first version dates to the days of "trial by ordeal," when justice was meted out by the gentle process of putting the accused into a huge pot of hot water and letting him boil his way to his fate and his maker. Undeniably, one who was unable to survive a roiling boil did indeed "go to pot."

But another version holds that "go to pot" refers to becoming an incurable drunkard. In olden times drinking men took their liquor straight and guzzled it out of huge earthenware pots. So to be "potted" was to be a dead drunk, and to "go to pot" was to have become a habitual drinker.

Justice Is Blind

From recent diggings in Egypt we've discovered that the early pharaohs were concerned with the administration of justice. Egyptian trials were crude, as we might expect, but in one particular way they might have been superior to a modern courtroom. In an attempt to avoid passion and prejudice, cases were tried in dark chambers. The Egyptians believed that when all the actors in a trial—the prisoner, the lawyers, and the judge—could not see each other, the judge would not be moved by anything other than the facts. Thus his judgment would be impartial.

Many who use the phrase today do so ironically, pointing out travesties in our judicial system. Perhaps these same critics would agree that such cases should be retried in dark courtrooms.

Sober as a Judge

While some might believe this expression originated because judges were thought to be beyond alcoholic impropriety, the exact opposite is true.

In the writings of Valerius Maximus is found a tale of Philip of Macedon that is the basis for this phrase. One of

Philip's female subjects appeared before him to be judged after he had been drinking heavily, and he found her guilty. But she managed to get her case resubmitted, and on her second appearance Philip, who was by then sober, acquitted her. He had failed to recognize her from her first appearance. All of which gave the lady pause to think and inspired the cynical reproach "as sober as a judge."

Hue and Cry

A great hullabaloo over nothing is a "hue and cry." This expression is almost as old as the English language itself; it once referred to a practice in England that made it next to impossible for a thief to get away with the loot.

In ancient England the country was divided into districts that could muster at least one hundred soldiers, which led each of these districts to be called a Hundred. Each district was considered a governmental unit and established its own court. If a crime was committed within its confines, it was the duty of the Hundred to apprehend the felon for the Crown. If the crime was a robbery, then the Hundred was responsible for the stolen property if the thief was not apprehended. Consequently, when a crime was committed, the victim or a person with firsthand knowledge of the crime would raise an outcry that was picked up by all the residents. The outcries continued until the whole community was assembled, a posse formed, and the criminal seized. This whole procedure was called the "hue and cry" of the Hundred.

Burning Question of the Day

When two learned people meet, one might greet the other with the query, "What's the burning question of the day?" By this she means, "What is the chief issue before us today that we need to discuss?"

In the days when church and state were one, if a person did not profess the religion of the state, she was guilty of treason by heresy. The penalty for heresy was death by burning. The writ issued in such cases was called "De Heretico Comburendo" (pertaining to the burning of a heretic).

When popular will began to clamor for separation of church and state, those who championed religious freedom were considered guilty of heresy, and many were seized and burned to death. Because of the many burnings, the great question of the day—namely freedom of worship—was called the "burning question."

When church and state were eventually separated, the writ "De Heretico Comburendo" was repealed and abolished. Religious freedom was recognized as a human right, as was the right to popular discussion of important public issues. Ever since, any vital issue that requires free and open discussion has been labeled the "burning question of the day."

Willy-Nilly

If you are compelled to do something against your will, you might say that you did it "willy-nilly." But did you know that when you use this phrase, you are alluding to the wheels of justice as they were understood in the era of common law?

Under common law, in order to get the wheels of justice into motion it was necessary to get the court to issue some kind of writ. One of the most frequently sought writs was that of "Nolens Volens," which, freely translated, is a writ of "not willing." Whenever anyone was taken into custody against his will, it was via a writ of "Nolens Volens." These writs were issued with such frequency in cases involving petty disturbances of the peace or minor legal infractions that they became known as Nilly-Willy Writs. And from this nickname we inherited our phrase "willy-nilly."

Pay Through the Nose

When we make unpleasant payments, such as taxes or bad bargains, we often say that we have "paid through the nose."

In the ninth century in Northern Ireland, a poll tax of one ounce of gold was imposed by England on all Irish households. The penalty for nonpayment was slitting the delinquent payer's nose. The tax was nicknamed the Nose Tax, and to avoid the penalty the Irish had to "pay through the nose."

Bigwig

The French court reveled in its greatest heights of pomp under Louis XIV. In his early years Louis XIV had long, flowing hair that he wore up, wig-style. Knowing his craving to set the fashion, his courtiers followed suit by wearing large, sumptuous wigs.

Other men of importance followed suit as "big wigs" became the fashion for prominent men. From France the style spread to the dignitaries of England—where lord chancellors, judges, and barristers still wear "big wigs." Bishops wore them in the House of Lords until 1880. The craze even spread to America. At one time there existed as many as forty different styles of men's wigs, among them the "Long Bob." After the craze passed, the last to wear wigs were those occupying important governmental posts. To these was attached the appellation "big wigs." Today all that remains from the wig obsession of years past is the phrase "bigwig," ironically used to describe those in the public eye who often seem impressed with their own importance.

Mind Your Ps and Qs

This phrase has two origins: one British, the other French.

The setting of the English story was the old-time bar. Here the bartender kept account of what patrons owed with Ps and Qs. Every P entered on the patron's tab represented one pint imbibed, and every Q stood for a quart. At settlement time the bartender would ask a customer to "mind his Ps and Qs," or to "bring to book," and to "pay up" according to the number of Ps and Qs on the account.

The French story comes once again from the court of Louis XIV. Remember the way male courtiers wore wigs of unwieldy size to please their monarch? Louis demanded that bows of obeisance be made to him with great formality. This was difficult when wearing a large wig, so to learn the art of bowing gracefully, the male courtiers took lessons at the Academy of the Royal Dancing Master. Here they were instructed on the necessary step with the feet and the low bend of the body required by the king. During the lessons, the wigs of the students would regularly fall off or become entangled in their feet. Hence the Royal Dancing Master would exhort his aristocratic charges to "mind their Ps and Qs" (*pieds* being French for "feet," and *queues* for "wigs").

Through the Mill

In commercial and legal circles "to go through the mill" means to go through bankruptcy. To the layman, it refers to any difficult and trying ordeal. Contrary to popular opinion, the phrase did not get its origin from the mechanics involved in operating lumber, paper, or cotton mills in early New England.

The phrase actually dates to the establishment of the first bankruptcy court in England. The first English bankruptcy law was called the Insolvent Debtor's Act. It provided for a court in which insolvent debtors could obtain legal discharge from their indebtedness by petition and proof of insolvency. The petitions were heard in a special court called the "Mill." Hence, the practice developed of referring to discharged bankrupts as people who had "gone through the Mill." Later the idiom took on the broad meaning in which it is used today.

Baker's Dozen

When you buy a dozen rolls and get thirteen, you have a "baker's dozen."

Baking was among the first industries subjected to governmental control and regulation. Soon after the baking profession was established, the king of England found it necessary to regulate it. The first public bakers put on the market unhealthy products of short weight and count. To fix this evil, exorbitant fines were imposed upon wayward bakers. The bakers, in response, and to ensure avoiding clashes with the law, gave thirteen to the dozen. From this practice we derived the happy "baker's dozen," an early example of government involvement in business.

A "baker's dozen" was also known as "a devil's dozen" because of "ye ancient baker's wizardry," which gave him the thirteenth chair (it belonged to the devil) at the Revel Table of the proverbial Twelve Witches. Even today, in the publishing trade in Scotland a "publisher's dozen" is thirteen books.

Poney Up

It is generally unpleasant to be compelled to "poney up." It does not mean to "saddle up," but rather to pay up or to make good on an obligation.

"Pone" (pronounced *poney*) was the name of a legal writ at common law, issued in the type of case where the bailiff was ordered to watch the defendant's goods or require security from the defendant to guarantee his personal appearance at the trail (today it is called "bail money"). "Pone" is derived from the Latin verb *ponere,* meaning to seize.

Cut the Red Tape

Bureaucratic and, as it turns out, legal delays derived their common phrase "red tape" deservedly.

For centuries, English kings put their royal decrees on parchment rolls bound with expensive red silk tape ribbons. When governmental bureaus were established, they mimicked the royal practice. Lawyers who sought royal or bureaucratic favors then followed suit by putting their written petitions in the same form. When Thomas Carlyle, the Scottish essayist and historian, and Charles Dickens wrote of governmental and legal delays, they called them "red tape." The phrase met with immediate public approval.

From Pillar to Post

Americans use the phrase "from pillar to post" to describe aimless effort. The phrase was inherited from a harsh, though quaint, custom of our Puritan ancestors.

The Puritans were a very moral set who dealt summarily with any of their group who dared deviate from their strict narrow code. All violators were first taken to the pillory, where, in full public view, their hands and feet were rigidly bound. The wrongdoers remained bound until they acknowledged the error of their ways. The unresponsive were led from the pillory, amid the shouting of the multitude, to the whipping post, where they were flogged. This generally achieved the desired result.

However, if the whipping post did not produce a promise of good future conduct, the victim was then cast out as "an incorrigible." The Puritans called this form of moral suasion "from pillar to post." Originally, it referred only to the fruitlessness of corporal punishment with incurable delinquents. Now its meaning embraces all forms of misdirected energy.

Straw Man

The term "straw man" refers to imaginary or figurative characters, usually conjured up to support a person's point in an argument.

Not so very many years ago in London there were found around the civil and criminal courts certain men who followed a most disreputable calling: They were "professional witnesses." For a cash consideration, they would give perjured testimony at trials. To indicate their base profession to litigants in need of doctored testimony, they walked about the corridors of law courts displaying a wisp of straw in their shoes. From the foot badges they wore, professional witnesses came to be called "straw men."

The modern "straw boss" derives his name from the same source.

Kick the Bucket

To "kick the bucket" means "to die." But why? Some say that the idiom goes back to the time when executions were public events.

A crowd would gather around a sturdy tree, a rope was attached to a strong branch, and the victim was placed atop an upturned water bucket. The noose was tied, and the executioner "kicked the bucket" from under the victim. You know the rest.

Others believe that the idiom's use predates hangings and arose from an accidental event that often occurred during the slaughter of farm animals. When a heavy animal, such as a steer, was slaughtered, a special hoist was employed. The dead steer's hind feet were bound with a rope, and the animal was pulled upward toward a beam at the top of a three-legged frame. A heavy wooden bucket was then shoved under the animal to collect the blood that drained from its body. As an animal was hoisted, its feet would often knock against the bucket, causing it to tip over and spill its bloody contents.

Bad Egg

So you think this expression came from the phenomenon that every once in a while you purchase a dozen eggs only to find that one of them is spoiled? You're wrong. Its origin is an example of the truth of a statement by Pliny the Younger (*Epistles,* early second century), who said, "The popularity of a bad man is as treacherous as he is himself."

Once there was an American named Egg who was a notorious criminal. The law caught up with him, and after paying the penalty, he could never regain the esteem of his neighbors. Indeed, they dubbed him "Bad Egg." The poor man died branded this way. Despite Egg's criminality, he still contributed to Americana: From his nickname have followed:

Tough egg
Rotten egg
Fresh egg
Hard-boiled egg

Stool Pigeon

This phrase is used as a derogatory label for a criminal who "ratted" (gave information) on his colleagues to the police, usually in exchange for a lighter jail sentence. But it used to be that all dishonest people were called "stool pigeons."

Not so many years ago the pigeon was an important item in every household food cabinet. Livestock animals were not abundant, and hunting for pigeons was not an autumn sport but crucial to human survival. It was discovered that pigeons could be lured into a net by placing a clay pigeon atop a pole called a stool. When the pigeons surrounded the decoy on the stool, they were covered with a net. The decoy was thus called a stool pigeon. Because the stool pigeon was used to deceive its victims, liars and similar malcontents were also called "stool pigeons."

Jailbird

A habitual criminal who has served several terms in prison is known as a "jailbird." The general public, however, may label anyone who has served a prison term the same way.

Primitive jails were initially large iron cages kept outdoors. They could house only a few prisoners at a time. These cages were portable and shaped like large birdcages. Because of their similarity, these ancient iron prisons were called cages. When they became known, in Britain, as gaols and later as jails, those thrown into them were referred to as "jailbirds." Although the modern jail is a far cry from the iron cages of the past, the unfortunate "jailbirds" who are housed within have not changed much in form.

Drawn, Hanged, and Quartered

To be humiliated completely is to be "drawn, hanged, and quartered." This phrase, although sufficiently severe in its implications today, was far more devastating in its effect when first used. It originated when treason was more commonplace than murder and when executions by hanging were the daily routine.

When a defendant was found guilty of treason and stood before the bar of justice to hear the sentence pronounced, the judge would drone out, "The defendant is hereby ordered to be *drawn*, *hanged*, and *quartered*." Thereupon, the criminal was "drawn" to the place of execution, "hung" on a gallows, and his corpse hewn into four "quarters." Each quarter was attached to a spike and hung up in four parts of a public place so that four times as many onlookers would be able to witness what happened to traitors.

By Hook or by Crook

When spared from serious difficulty, we have been saved "by hook or by crook."

In feudal England every serf had what was called a Forestal Right by Hook or Crook. The hook and the crook were both long poles. The former had a sharp point on which things could be hooked, while the latter had a semicircular end by which things could be held. The law stated that any serf could enter the forestal lands and remove branches or timber that could be gathered in with the "hook or crook." The use of an ax or saw violated the law and was punishable by the feudal lord. When feudalism collapsed and the serf no longer needed these two tools to survive, the phrase lived on. "Hook" and "Crook" were even taken as family names. And during the Great Fire of London in 1666, in which more than twelve thousand houses were burned and destroyed, the British government appointed two experienced land surveyors by the names of Hook and Crook to determine the rights of various claimants to disputed lands. Their fair treatment of claimants kept this common phrase alive.

Go to Halifax

It may not be very elegant to tell a person to "go to Halifax," but it's often very effective. It is not, however, a profane expression, but one with an interesting geographic and historical background.

Halifax, one of the oldest of English cities, is located in the Yorkshire district. Years ago Halifax was noted for the severity of its criminal law; the common law maxim, "A man is presumed to be innocent until proved guilty," did not exist there. The Halifax practice was to condemn a criminal first and inquire about his guilt later. In some cases, particularly punishments that carried the death penalty, that was a bit too late to help the accused.

If the victim was found innocent, however, his family and descendants would not be required to suffer further for his crimes, as was the practice in Europe at the time. The descendants of a man convicted of heresy, for example, could never hold rank in the military, hold public office, or acquire land. For years family members would expend huge sums of money to prove their forefather's innocence.

Still, it was the law of Halifax: "If a felon were taken with thirteen and a half pence worth of goods stolen from within Halifax, he should be tried by four burghers from four of the town precincts, and if condemned by them, be hanged next market day, after which the case might be sent to the jury."

No small wonder, then, that "go to Halifax" became a popular expression in England. Now it is used by English-speaking people everywhere who want somebody sent to a place where they will be dealt with summarily.

Give It the Lie

There is only one thing to do when you're charged mistakenly and untruthfully with doing something wrong, and that is to "give it the lie." This is an Anglo-Saxon phrase of ancient origin, traced back to a period in English history when one of the most popular forms of lawsuit was "trial by combat."

For a judicial combat to be legal in feudal days, an austere procedure—almost as formal and technical as our modern "code pleading" or "plea bargaining," as it is now more popularly called—had to be followed. First, the knight who thought himself wronged would publicly take an oath and charge the defendant with having committed the wrong. Then the defending knight would publicly take an oath, directed at the plaintiff, denying the plaintiff's charge.

The defendant's oath of denial began with the words, "Thou liest." This denial was called "giving the lie." After it was given, the knights dueled. The winner of the duel was declared the truthful and innocent party.

Trial by combat, like trial by ordeal before it, has given way to trial by jury, but "to give it the lie" is still an important part of our code of chivalry.

Go to Coventry

There are many who believe that the idiom "to go to Coventry" contains an allusion to man's covenant with God, stressed in the Old Testament.

The Coventry referred to in this phrase, however, was the undesirable region of Coventry, England. When Oliver Cromwell overthrew Charles II and established an English protectorate, all of the Royalists whom Cromwell captured were sent to a prison that Cromwell had established at Coventry. These Royalist prisoners were treated none too easily, and tales of Coventry's horrific punishments reached other English cities by word of mouth. As a result, the phrase "go to Coventry" became synonymous with merciless punishment.

Lay by the Heels

To render someone powerless is to "lay by the heels." At
first glance it's difficult to see what connection a person's
heels might have to do with her strength. To understand
this phrase, we must recall a quaint form of corporal punishment used extensively in the days when America was
first colonized.

You may remember our earlier discussion of how Pilgrim
fathers put an offender against the public morals in the pillory, also known as the stocks. These were crude structures
made of wood and designed to hold several prisoners in sitting positions with their feet protruding through circular
openings so that their heels were in public view. Not only
was this posture most painful to the victim, but it gave rise to
the expression "lay by the heels." Try "laying by the heels"
and you'll quickly see that, in such a posture, you're powerless.

Wave the Bloody Shirt

A favorite device of the political demagogue is to "wave the
bloody shirt"—that is, to get the masses behind him by ap-
pealing to base prejudices and passions. Today "wave the
bloody shirt" is just a figure of speech, but there was a time
when this phrase was taken literally.

It was a custom of the Corsicans to avenge the violent
death of the head of a family by murdering the murderer.
The game of murder for murder was called the Vendetta,
and its practice so seriously set Corsican families against
each other that tranquility was the exception and murder the

rule. Before burying a victim of the Vendetta, his family would celebrate a Gridata, a type of funeral wake.

The victim's body was placed upon a board, his weapons of defense placed alongside, and his hands and head covered with his blood-stained shirt. Around the bier sat the female mourners, wrapped heavily in their dark black mantles. The male mourners, fully armed, stood around the room. Soon the women, rocking to and fro, would begin wailing and demanding vengeance. At the height of the wailing the widow of the deceased, with a frenzied scream, would snatch her husband's bloody shirt and wave it aloft to the cries of the mourners, while the men would pledge vengeance. Then a dirge was chanted and burial would take place.

In the United States during and immediately after the Civil War, to "wave the bloody shirt" was to refer to the sectional issues of the war in such a way as to stir up bloodshed.

Pay (or Stand) the Racket

To "pay (or stand) the racket" is an ancient phrase that dates to the beginning of Anglo-Saxon law.

Among the early Anglo-Saxons of Scotland and England, when blood feuds were common, the legal practice of "rachet" (pronounced *racket*) was established in an effort to outlaw feuding. If a man was murdered as a result of a family feud, the family of the murderer was compelled to pay a ransom to the family of the victim. The ransom was a fine large enough to recompense the wrongful death; when it was paid, the murderer would be returned to his family.

This practice was in Scotland called "standing the rachet." In England it later was named "weregild."

Over time the "rachet" principle was extended to all crimes in which the victim suffered property losses. Thus, the family of a thief was required to "pay the rachet" in an amount equal to the value of the stolen loot so the prisoner could be returned to his family. "Rachet" eventually became "Racket" and the practice was known as "paying the racket." With the development of common law, "paying the racket" gave way to punishment by imprisonment or, in capital crimes, death.

Today the phrase has evolved to describe a victim who "pays the racket" by paying tribute to avoid terrorism or violence of racketeering mobsters.

4
Cardinal Sins

 Here we present common phrases that evolved from religious experiences. Some of these idioms predate the birth of Christ, while others reflect the anatomical naïveté of the period.

Doubting Thomas

A person who is very hard to convince is referred to as a "doubting Thomas."

Among the disciples of Jesus was one man who refused to believe in Christ's resurrection. That disciple was Thomas. Because of his doubts, he was called "the doubting or very Thomas." Since then, a person who doubts and hesitates unnecessarily on matters about which others have no doubts is said to be a "doubting Thomas" or "very Thomas."

By the Skin of the Teeth

Teeth have no skin. Yet someone who has narrowly escaped from peril has "escaped by the skin of her teeth."

It was the devout biblical character Job who coined the phrase. In Job 29:20 is found: "I have escaped with the skin of my teeth!" Job lived long before the use of toothpaste and therefore must be excused for having confused the tartar on his teeth with human skin!

Adam's Apple

The prominent lump in the human throat took its name, "Adam's apple," from an old superstitious belief.

Everyone is familiar with the story of Adam and Eve. But what many people might not be acquainted with is how the Bible story was actually embellished. It was said that when Adam swallowed the forbidden fruit, one large piece of the apple remained in his throat and formed a lump there. The lump in every man's throat was named for the very first man, and so the "Adam's apple" was born.

Rob Peter to Pay Paul

If the owner of a baseball team trades the team's star player in order to free up funds to hire another player, or destroys team morale by giving an unusually high salary to an unproven player, baseball fans may say the owner has "robbed Peter to pay Paul." The saying applies to the puzzling behavior of any individual who exchanges property of known value for that of questionable or unknown value.

On December 17, 1740, a Royal Letters Patent was issued in England making the Abbey Church of St. Peter, London, a cathedral. At the same time the diocese of St. Paul's Cathedral was experiencing considerable financial difficulty. So badly strained was the treasury that the powers that be decided to merge St. Paul's with St Peter's. Consequently, a new Royal Letters Patent was issued in 1750, and St. Paul's absorbed St. Peter's. The funds of the former St. Peter's were used solely to pay for badly needed repairs at St. Paul's Cathedral. The parishioners of St. Peter's resented this, and from out of their protests came the rallying cry of "robbing Peter to pay Paul."

True Blue

To be extremely loyal is to be "true blue."

"A true Covenanter wears true blue" was one of the slogans of the Scottish Covenanters during their seventeenth-century struggles with King Charles I. Covenanters were Presbyterians who supported either the National Covenant of 1638 or the Solemn League and Covenant of 1643, both intended to defend and extend Presbyterianism. They took blue as their official color because of the religious practice of observing the scriptural language literally.

According to Numbers 15:38, "Speak to the children of Israel and tell them to make to themselves fringes of the borders of their garments, putting in them ribbons of blue." Arrayed in "true blue," the Covenanters carried the day, and ever since the phrase "true blue" has symbolized the noblest human qualities.

Cock and Bull Story

This phrase originated in the aftermath of the Reformation of the sixteenth century in which papal bulls (decrees) and Martin Luther's bulls played such important roles.

72

After Luther had issued his famous bulls, which were the declarations of faith of the New Church, his followers scorned the bulls issued by the Pope. On the papal bulls were seals imprinted with the Pope's bulla, a stamp bearing the likeness of St. Peter accompanied by the cock that, according to legend, had crowed three times when it disowned its master.

Before long Luther's disciples referred to anything that they did not believe as being "cock and bull." With the growth and expansion of the Reformation, this phrase was picked up by peoples of all faiths and countries.

When in Rome, Do as the Romans Do

One of the first great men in history to recognize the social value of majority rule was the famous churchman St. Augustine.

When St. Augustine dispatched St. Ambrose from Milan to Rome, Ambrose was perplexed about the proper day on which to fast, for, in Rome, it was then the custom to fast on Saturday. He asked St. Augustine which fast day to observe. The learned Augustine remarked, "When in Rome, do as the Romans do." Because these words of St. Augustine were both wise and practical, they have become one of the world's noblest maxims.

Talking Through Your Hat

If a person's facts are incorrect, we charge him with "talking through his hat."

This phrase comes from an English custom dating back to around 1850. Prior to that time, no worshiper would dare fail to kneel and utter a short prayer before sitting down at a pew. But one fastidious Englishman, not wanting to soil his trousers by kneeling, thought it sufficient to simply hold his hat in front of his face and, while standing, say a prayer before taking his pew. Others imitated the man, who "prayed through his hat." This practice became widespread, and it so shocked the reverent that they called it "talking through your hat." Before long "talking through your hat" was employed to describe any talk that was irreverent, insincere, or false.

Cheating the Devil

When someone successfully emerges from a dangerous and difficult situation unscathed, we often say that she is "cheating the devil."

Two classic tales gave birth to this phrase. The first appears in the Hebrew Talmud, where it is related that a man entered into a compact with the devil. In return for granting abundant crops, the devil was to get the crops that grew under the soil one year; the next year he would get the crops that grew above the soil. During the devil's above-the-soil year, the farmer raised carrots and turnips. In the below-the-soil year, he raised wheat and barley. Thus the man "cheated the devil."

Longfellow, in his "Golden Legend," tells a similar story. An abbot contracted with the devil for the construction of a bridge over the falls of a river. The abbot agreed to give the devil the first living thing that crossed over the bridge after the devil completed it. When the bridge was done, the wise abbot threw a loaf of bread across the river, and a hungry dog crossed the bridge in pursuit of the bread. Thus, again, the man "cheated the devil."

By the Elevens

The number eleven is used in a profane manner in this common phrase because it is the first number after ten and indicative of those who have broken the Ten Commandments. Among this group, twelve is the proper symbol of the good and the just, because it represents the twelve apostles.

Black Friday

Originally "black Friday" took its name from the black vestments worn by clergy at Good Friday services and applied to only one Friday of each year, namely the Friday preceding Easter Sunday. Yet owing to coincidences in both the United States and England, the phrase has taken on another meaning, far removed from anything religious. In financial circles "black Friday" is a specific reference to certain days of financial panics, and a general name for those too-frequent days on which investors suffer heavy losses.

The first "black Friday" was on December 6, 1745, in England, after news reached there that Charles Edward Stuart, the Young Pretender (to the British throne), had arrived in Derby. These tidings caused panic, and gigantic losses resulted. The second "black Friday" occurred on May 11, 1866, when the Banking-House of Overend, Gurney and Company, closed its doors, causing widespread ruin in England's financial centers.

On Friday, September 26, 1869, the United States suffered its first "black Friday" when Jay Gould and his associates tried to corner the entire gold market. Panic ensued until the secretary of the treasury eased the market by releasing four million dollars in gold. The last American "black Friday" occurred on September 19, 1873, the beginning of the financial panic of the same year.

With Benefit of Clergy

If an act is approved of socially, we may say that it was done "with benefit of clergy." The origin of this phrase dates back to the days when there were two courts in England—civil court and the church-sponsored courts.

In the civil courts the penalty for certain crimes was death. The church-sponsored courts were less severe; death penalties were never handed down. Initially, whether a person was tried by a church or a civil court depended upon his ability to prove a blood relationship with a clergyman. Later, all those who could read were entitled to "benefit of clergy," which put them under the jurisdiction of the church courts. The first verse of the Psalm 51 was chosen as the reading test, and became known as the "neck verse" because it saved the neck of many a criminal who could read it.

Prickings of Conscience

When you have erred, the uncomfortable aftereffects of your wrongdoing are called the "prickings of conscience." It's hard to believe, then, that a hermit was the first to coin this phrase.

In 1350 Richard Rolle, a hermit who dwelled beyond the environs of Hampole, England, wrote a celebrated text about solitary thought. He titled it *The Prick of Conscience*. This treatise was a best-seller for the time, and soon "prickings of conscience" became a popular phrase.

Never Look Back

This phrase's origin can be traced to the Old Testament and the tragic story of Lot's wife, who, contrary to the orders of the guiding angel who was supervising Lot's household, looked back and was transformed into a pillar of salt.

Among the Hindustan, it was considered an ill omen to look back after leaving your house. A dutiful Hindustan's wife never dared send her husband back into the house to get something she had left behind. She knew that if he went back, he would not set forth again for fear of terrible consequences.

Anxious Seat

Salespeople say they are on the "anxious seat" when they wait outside a prospect's office. People awaiting important tidings refer to the waiting period as the "anxious seat," particularly prospective fathers.

The phrase comes from old-fashioned Methodist camp revival meetings. At these meetings benches were reserved for the penitents who were conscious of having sinned. These seats, set apart from the others, were called the "anxious benches." After the regular service, the "anxious service" was held for the relief of those on the special benches. When they atoned for all their wrongs, they were readmitted to membership, and their anxiety was supplanted by faith.

5
Rigmarole

 While the first idiom listed below could have been included earlier in the book, it seemed fitting to include it in this chapter on politics. Much of what constituted ancient politics was the act of killing one leader and replacing him with another. Only much later did politics become the complicated set of procedures or the "rigmarole" that we know today. Incidentally, the term "rigmarole" itself came from the words *ragemane rolle,* a scroll used in ragman, a medieval game of chance. What does that tell you about how little politics have changed?

Stab in the Back

Today we refer to unkind words or a cowardly action as a "stab in the back." Yet when this phrase first came into use, it alluded, most pointedly, to a dagger or sword stabbed into a person's back with the intent to murder him.

A common misconception is that this phrase originated from Julius Caeser's assassination. Actually, the first fatal "stab in the back" in recorded history, and the derivation of the phrase, dates back to the Saxon king Edward the Martyr.

Elfrida wanted Edward out of the way so she could seize the throne. By prearrangement with an assassin, when Edward was taking a cup of wine from Elfrida's servant, poor Edward, with his backed turned, was stabbed in the back. A new sovereign took the throne and gave to history the "stab in the back."

Spill the Beans

"To reveal a secret" is the most popular meaning of "spill the beans." The phrase comes from the ancient Greeks, among whom beans were very important not only for food but also in the conduct of their local elections.

When a Greek voted, his ballot was cast by putting a bean in the helmet of the candidate of his choice whose helmet lay alongside those of the whole slate of candidates. The candidate whose helmet had the greatest number of beans in it at the close of the election was declared the winner. The count was public, and when the winner was announced, his helmet, with the beans in it, was returned to him. Thereupon, he would "spill the beans" out of the helmet and, amid the applause of the voters, put it on his head. This act symbolized his acceptance of the office to which he had been elected. Because the helmet contained the outcome of the election, "spill the beans" became synonymous with disclosing a secret, which is the way we use the phrase today.

Taking the Blue Ribbon

Have you ever wondered why the "blue ribbon" is the symbol of champions?

Blue was the favorite color of King Edward III of England. In 1348, by royal act, Edward III created the Royal Order of Knights of the Garter and proclaimed it the highest royal order in Great Britain, a position it still holds today.

Originally its membership was limited to the king, the princes of England, and twenty-five royal companion knights. The order has since been enlarged to include sovereigns and princes of foreign lands and a limited number of knights selected for distinguished service. The insignia of the order is, as originally declared by Edward III, "A Garter of Blue Ribbon." The people subsequently made this royal symbol a mark of distinction. The practice continues today, and when we say that something "takes the blue ribbon," we mean that the feat or creation is supreme and champion of its class.

As a side note, in England the Blue Ribbon of the Church is worn by the archbishop of Canterbury and the Blue Ribbon of Law by the lord chancellor, who is comparable to the chief justice of the Supreme Court in the United States.

I'll Be Hanged If I Do

Thelwall was an English poet of liberal political views. He disagreed violently with King George III's tyrannical rule, helped organize the Jacobin Societies in 1791, and was an active worker in the Society of Friends. He wrote and lectured against the king and supported the cause of American independence. During a lecture at the Capel Court Society, he "likened a crowned despot to a bantam cock or a dunghill." This caught the fancy of radicals of the day and, not surprisingly, enraged the king.

On May 13, 1764, Thelwall, along with thirty-two other rebels, was arrested for "having moved a seditious resolution" at a meeting at Chalk Farm. He was held at Newgate prison until his trial. While at Newgate he wrote a number of fiery poems that were published in 1795. At the start of his trial Thelwall sent a note to his counsel, the famous Erskine, on which was written, "I shall be hanged if I don't plead my own cause." Erskine returned the note, "You'll be hanged if you do." Thelwall replied, "I'll be hanged if I do." Thelwall was acquitted, and through Erskine the public learned of Thelwall's "I'll be hanged if I do" line. It became the slogan of the liberal cause and had much to do with the final undoing of King George III.

On the Fence

A great American phrase is "on the fence," expressing indecision. It gained popularity as a result of its use by George Washington, who picked it up from a slave.

During the New Jersey campaign of the Revolutionary War, many were undecided about who to support. The followers of the revolutionary cause were called Whigs, and the British sympathizers Tories. There was some doubt about the sympathizers led by Judge Imlay, a prominent New Jersey jurist. Washington met a slave of Judge Imlay on the highway. He asked him whether the judge was Whig or Tory. The reply was, "Massa's on de fence; him want to know which de strongest party." Washington was amused by "on de fence" and related the incident to numerous friends. Over repeated tellings, "on de fence" became "on the fence."

Take a Back Seat

Some believe this phrase originated with the rumble seats in early automobiles, but it actually dates back much earlier.

President Andrew Johnson, the first American president against whom impeachment proceedings were initiated, tried to institute Abraham Lincoln's program of Reconstruction after the Civil War. In a message outlining his position Johnson said, "In the work of Reconstruction, traitors should 'take back seats.' " Although the carpetbaggers and corruptionists of Johnson's day did not "take back seats," the public has taken Johnson's expression to heart and still uses it appropriately.

Mend Fences

The expression "mending fences" means "to make amends" or "to apologize to those we have wronged." Among politicians, success at the polls often depends on how well a candidate has "mended her fences."

The phrase originated in the presidential campaign of 1880. John Sherman, an Ohio senator at the time, left Washington while Congress was in session for his farm near Mansfield, Ohio. It was rumored that he'd retired to his farm in order to confer secretly with Republican political leaders and elicit their support for his candidacy for president. One day while he was on his farm with his friend

Colonel Moulton, a political reporter found Sherman and Moulton mending a fence. The reporter, bent on a scoop, asked what Sherman was doing. Colonel Moulton, answering for Sherman, said, "Why you can see for yourself, he's mending his fences." The reporter made "mending fences" the feature of his story, and the phrase has been in popular use ever since.

Red Herring

The great indoor sport of politicians while campaigning is to harangue over matters totally irrelevant to the real issues. This form of demagoguery was first called "dragging a red herring across the trail," and later condensed to simply "red herring."

The phrase was first applied by philosophers to a scholar who tried to prove a thesis by arguments not logically connected to it. These wise men would be shocked to know that this phrase comes from the artful practice of absconding criminals of yore, who, to cover their tracks, used a strong-smelling smoked red herring. Its use would mask their scent to the bloodhounds that pursued them. For many years afterward, hunting dogs and bloodhounds were trained to discriminate between false and true scents by the use of smoked red herrings.

Gerrymander

It is an old political practice for a legislative body to divide up the election districts of the electorate in the manner that will best serve the interests of the political party in power. The name for this political abuse is "gerrymandering."

This phrase obtained its name from a former governor of Massachusetts, Elbridge Gerry, who later became vice president under James Madison. While governor, Gerry forced the state legislature, the majority of whom were members of his political party, to subdivide the commonwealth of Massachusetts into election districts that isolated Federalist strongholds and ensured Republican domination in subsequent elections.

When a map showing the new electoral distribution was shown to the state artist for reproduction, he remarked that one of the new election districts looked "very much like a salamander." The reply he received was, "A salamander, you say? A Gerrymander, you mean, don't you?"

Take the Stump

When a political candidate makes a speaking tour during a political campaign, we say that he has "taken the stump."

Early political campaigns in the United States, particularly the presidential campaigns from 1820 to 1880, are among the most thrilling chapters in American history. In that era large regions of the United States were undeveloped, and the country abounded with forests. Men took their whiskey and their politics straight and raw.

Most political speeches were made in forest clearings. The candidates spoke from the largest tree stump in a clearing. A political meeting was an event to which backwoodsmen would travel over rough roads, in rickety wagons, and for long distances just to hear politicians debate from the "tree stumps."

Other political idioms originating from the same source include:

Stump speech
Stumping the country
Stumping the state
Stumping grounds
Stump speaker

All Talk and No Cider

Have you ever been to a dinner party where a group of intellectuals became so involved in their profound discussions that the evening ended without much attention being directed to the meal? What you experienced was "all talk and no cider."

A prominent citizen of Back County, Pennsylvania, invited a large group of friends to his home, telling them that he had a very large barrel of superior cider to serve to them. Whetted by the thought of the cider, a crowd gathered. To the surprise of the guests, political speeches instead of the cider barrel were rolled out, one after another, until the hour was late and there was no time for cider. The story circulated quickly, and the phrase became a popular way to describe a verbose but otherwise unproductive gathering.

Silk Stocking

It is no longer a mark of wealth or distinction to wear silk hosiery. But it wasn't too long ago that only people with large bank balances could wear silk stockings, and only at formal functions.

John Morrissey, a retired New York prizefighter, stepped from the prize ring into the political ring. Initially he was quite successful. Then, in 1876, a number of wealthy and fashionable men became interested in politics and decided to take over Morrissey's political party. This worried the rough-and-ready Morrissey, so one morning, attired in full evening dress and with a French dictionary under his arm, he paraded the streets of New York exclaiming to each passerby, "Things are coming to 'such a pass' in New York City that unless one wears swallow tails, silk stockings, and speaks polite French, he is not in politics." Morrissey's stunt worked, and, inspired by this dramatic coup, the public nicknamed the defeated power brokers "silk stockings."

Lobby

The term "lobbying" refers to any and every form of outside pressure or influence exerted upon legislators to affect their votes on legislation pending before them.

The phrase originated in England shortly after the British Parliament Building was unveiled. Parliament contains England's House of Lords and House of Commons, and the corridor between the Chamber of Lords and the Chamber of Commons—because it is extensive and because the general public was admitted to it—was called the Lobby. Here was where constituents would meet with their legislative representatives to discuss legislation whose passage or defeat was of interest to them.

Stand Sam

Politicians are also responsible for our phrase "to stand Sam," which means "to pay the check for refreshments."

It originated in Washington, and the Sam mentioned is of course Uncle Sam. Before the expenses of federal employees began to receive today's close scrutiny, it was common practice among high-level federal workers to wine and dine friends and relatives and to make Uncle Sam stand (or pay) for it by way of their expense accounts. From such abuse we get our expression "standing Sam."

Carry Coals to Newcastle

In times of crisis there are always some individuals who insist upon doing what is obviously the wrong thing, and then compound their folly by making a big show of it. In the same category are self-seekers who bear unnecessary gifts. Describing such people is the common phrase "he'd carry coals to Newcastle."

Newcastle was at one time the greatest coal market of the world. Even from its inception as a city, Newcastle was a great coal center. In 1239 the burgesses of the city obtained from Henry III royal authority to dig coal from its vicinity. By the reign of Edward I, the city of Newcastle was paying an annual tax on coal of more than two hundred pounds. In 1615 its coal dealers used more than four hundred ships to transport coal to France and the Netherlands. So "carrying coals to Newcastle" has long been an act of folly.

Log Rolling

"Log rolling" is an Americanism of legitimate origin put to illegitimate use by politicians. When America was colonized, it was the practice of early settlers to share their burdens. The first job to get a new settlement established was to clear a tract of forestland. Trees were chopped, cut into loads, and then rolled to a clearing, where they were used to build log cabins. The process of helping each other build cabins that everybody would use came to be called "log rolling."

After the American Revolution, some of our early legislators applied to their work the cooperative principle of "log rolling" by supporting each other's measures. "Log rolling" among the pioneers produced wholesome communities, while among legislators it produced the unwholesome "pork barrel."

A special type of "log rolling" became a sport. A log is placed in a lake, and lumberjacks take turns to see how long each can stand on the log while rolling it over and over with their feet. This contest is still conducted at fairs and special events, with prizes awarded to the winners.

Another County Heard From

Among Americans, the right to hold in contempt the opinion of another is guaranteed by the Constitution. "Another county heard from" is one way of saying this politely. Originally, however, this expression had a totally different meaning.

"Another county heard from" arose from the presidential campaign of 1876. The candidates were Tilden and Hayes, and as the returns came in, it became clear that the election would be very, very close. As each set of returns arrived in the various states from their county districts, the results would go back and forth. First Tilden would hold the lead, then Hayes. As results from a county were announced, Tilden's supporters would cry, "Another county heard from!" When all the counties had been heard from, Tilden was credited with the majority of the total popular vote. But Hayes was elected because he received the majority of the electoral votes. Thus, all the shouting by Tilden supporters was for nil. Hayes supporters shouted, "Another county heard from," derisively at the Tilden followers when the returns of the electoral vote were announced and Hayes won the presidency.

Given the events of the 2000 presidential election, the cry is still appropriate today. "Another county heard from" is also one of the most popularly used phrases to express either ridicule or contempt for the officious opinion of a neighbor.

I Don't Give a Continental

Impress your friends when you want to express contempt by saying, "I don't give a continental"—an admittedly archaic term.

During the Revolution, government was carried on by the Continental Congress. From time to time the Continental Congress issued paper money. When the tide of battle did not favor the revolutionary cause, this currency, called the continental, deflated substantially and became worthless. This led to the expression "I don't give a continental."

Let George Do It

If you want to push an unpleasant task upon somebody else, you might say, "Let George do it." The first to use this expression was no less than a king—Louis XII of France.

Louis XII's prime minister was Georges d'Amboise. He was both prime minister and the king's closest confidant, which gave him as much power as the king himself. Louis would not make a move unless it was approved of or urged by d'Amboise. Whenever the king was asked to do something, his reply was stock: *"Laissez-faire à Georges,"* which roughly translates to "Let George do it."

So frequently did Louis use this phrase that the court attendants picked it up. Jokingly, at first, they would say *"Laissez-faire à Georges"* whenever they wanted to shirk their duties. Through the courtiers, *"Laissez-faire à Georges"* circulated throughout France. When it crossed the English Channel, it was translated into its English equivalent, "Let George do it."

The phrase was revived when Lord George was at the height of his power and popularity in England. Since then it has continued to be popular in both England and America.

6
Handles

 "Trade talk" has resulted in a lot of common phrases. A person's trade is even referred to as his "handle," because so many trades involve operating or "handling" tools or machines.

Merchants, fishermen, liverymen, butchers, printers, carpenters, miners, lumbermen, industrialists, entertainers, and particularly seamen introduced many common phrases that not only transcended their trade but remain in use today.

Some of the phrases in this chapter arose from the movement in the mid–nineteenth century to change lifestyle and to seek fortunes elsewhere by migrating West. While these phrases don't necessarily involve a trade, they do involve a livelihood, which is why we've chosen to include them here.

Earmark It

If you want to identify something clearly, or if you're trying to retain a fact in your memory, you will be sure to "earmark it." Yet chances are high that what you want to identify or remember has no ears, so how did this common phrase originate?

The answer dates back to a practice of old English herdsmen. They knew nothing of branding cattle, yet they realized the necessity of identifying their herds, particularly in those parts of England where cattle grazed in the commons—pastures shared by numerous herds. So they slit or notched the ears of their animals. While this may have been painful for the cattle, it was convenient for the herders. From this ancient practice of "earmarking" cattle, we obtained our expression "earmark it."

Spick and Span

Before rulers and yardsticks, the most extensively used units of measurement were the "spick," deriving its name from the spick-nail (which, if measured today, would be two and a quarter inches), and the "span," which was the length of the average extended hand from the thumb to the little finger. If computed today from the average hand, the "span" would be about nine inches.

The "spick" and "span" came into popular use when tailors measured their patrons for tailor-made garments. The "spick" was used for bust or chest measurements, and the "span" for length. New garments were cut according to "spicks" and "spans," and the measurements were so clean and precise that the phase "spick and span" gradually came to be synonymous with "neat and tidy."

Pretty Kettle of Fish

This phrase has been popular ever since William the Conqueror took over England in 1066. Shortly after the Norman Conquest, one of the chief industries of England was fishing. To carry on his work, the early fisherman used a kiddelus, also called kiddle. Even in the Magna Carta, there is a clause that guarantees the "kiddelus rights" of fishermen.

The kiddelus was an arrangement of nets thrown into the sea; when it was pulled out filled with fish it took on a kettlelike appearance. The sight of a kiddelus full of squirming fish, while a bounty to the grateful fishermen, was also quite a chaotic scene; hence "pretty kettle of fish" came to mean "chaos."

The term *kittle* also means "to puzzle or perplex." The perplexing confusion of fish, when caught, was first observed by Scottish fishermen. "Kittle of fish" was a common phrase for a bewildering fact, and by usage "kittle" became "kettle."

Hang Out

When you ask your kids about what they're going to do over at their friends' houses that they can't do at home, the answer you may get is that they're just gonna "hang out." Little do they know that this expression originated with one of the earliest commercial practices in England.

All "hangouts" have one thing in common: They are places where men and women assemble to pass the time in gossip, play, and fellowship. In old Humphrey Bogart movies the "hangout," usually called the "hideout," was where gangsters assembled to pass the time between robberies and plan their next venture.

Long before business signs were used, early English shopkeepers set up poles in the middle of the road in front of their shops. On these poles they would "hang out" flags bearing inscriptions describing their wares. The townsfolk would gather around these poles to read what was written on each "hangout." Often they would idle and linger around the "hangout" to talk and gossip with their friends. Soon these "hangouts" became regular meeting places. While neon signs have replaced this method of advertising, the "hangout" is still one of our most popular institutions.

Queer Street

While the word *queer* has been a derogatory term associated with individuals who are sexually attracted to members of their own sex (currently referred to as gay), its original use "sprang up" from a very different source. The idiom "to be in Queer Street" means "to be refused credit."

The phrase originated among English tradesmen. If a person's credit was doubtful, then the word *query,* meaning "doubt," would be entered after his name in his creditor's ledger. When exchanging credit information with each other, the tradesmen would call their delinquent accounts "queries." Soon the buying public learned the significance of the merchants' "query" and said of an insolvent that "he was queried in the business streets"—later shortened to "he's in Queer Street."

Put the Kibosh on It

To put an end to a pointless or endless discussion is the literal meaning of the phrase "put the kibosh on it."

In old England, on Petticoat Lane, there were numerous auction stores whose owners and patrons were Dutch Jewish refugees who had escaped to England to avoid religious persecution. They knew little English and did their trading in Yiddish, a dialect made up of Hebrew and German words and phrases. *Kibosh* was the Yiddish word for "eighteen half-pence" or "nine pennies," a relatively insignificant sum. When an eager bidder wanted to cut short the bidding on a petty article, he would cry out, "Kibosh." The bidding would stop and the article would promptly be sold to him.

Get Down to Brass Tacks

From Main Street to Wall Street, "Let's get down to brass tacks" refers to getting down to work to finish the business at hand. This phrase originated from an old practice in the retail dry-goods business.

Before machines were invented to measure and cut the yard goods sold in retail stores, every dry-goods merchant had at least one counter where business was transacted. Along this counter's edge, brass tacks were placed at quarter-yard intervals. These brass tacks were indispensable as measurement instruments, and a merchant knew that when his customer told him to use the brass tacks to measure off a quantity of material, he had made a sale. Hence, he was anxious to hurdle the preliminaries and "get down to brass tacks."

Hobson's Choice

To have no choice is to have a "Hobson's choice." It was a personal eccentricity that evolved into this figure of speech, which now has an international following.

Thomas Hobson operated a livery stable in Cambridge, England, from about 1580 until his death in 1631. While there is nothing noteworthy about the average liveryman, Hobson was a doggedly unique renter of horses. Not even the Prince of Wales could be assured of renting the horse of his choice, for it was Hobson's iron-clad rule that each customer took the horse nearest to the door. In this way Hobson, who was very fond of all his horses, could ensure that no horse worked harder than another.

Because Hobson had the best horses in all Cambridge, the enforcement of his rule did not injure his business. Indeed, his rule not only enhanced Hobson's livelihood but also gave the world the picturesque phrase "Hobson's choice."

Save the Bacon

If you survive an experience in which your life was endangered, you're said to have "saved the bacon."

Before there were supermarkets, if you wanted bacon you had to slaughter your own pig and then remove the bristle from the swine's hide. This task was performed by singeing, a process that required delicate handling. Too much singeing would ruin the bacon, and since singeing happened so commonly, it was considered a deft mix of skill and luck to "save the bacon."

Out of Sorts

While it's too much to expect that everyone will always be in tiptop shape, why is it that when folks aren't "up to par," we say they're "out of sorts"? For our answer we turn to the printing trade.

Here we find "sorts" to be integral pieces of type necessary to make up what printers call a font of type. When a printer's supply of "sorts" is exhausted, no work can be done until this supply is replenished. There are various tales of the antics of irritated printers when they run out of sorts. The more conscientious printers were about getting work out without delay, the more distressed they became when the "sorts" ran out!

Get the Sack

To "get the sack" or "get sacked" means "to be fired from your job." In the world of romance and soft caresses it means "to be disavowed." In war a "sacked" village has been destroyed by its conquerors. Small wonder, then, at the legend that "sack" was the last word uttered at the

Tower of Babel when all the languages of the human tongue were scrambled. The word "sack" is found in more languages than any other word linguists have encountered.

Before the industrial era, workers carried their tools in sacks. When an employer discharged a worker, he simply handed him his sack. The worker, knowing the custom, would put his tools in it and, with full sack across his back, march out to join the army of the unemployed.

The first lover "got the sack" in the sixteenth century when Emperor Maxmillian II paid his debt to two noblemen who had performed deeds of great valor for His Highness. Both had asked to marry his beautiful daughter, Helena. Maxmillian did not want to lose either of the suitors in a duel for his daughter's hand. Consequently, he ordered a large sack brought before him and proclaimed, "He who shall put his rival into the sack will win the hand of fair Helena." In the presence of the entire imperial court, the sack combat was enacted. It lasted several hours. Finally one nobleman "sacked" the other, took him sack and all on his back, laid the sack with its human contents at the feet of Maxmillian, and claimed his prize—the fair Helena. Ever since, ladies fair have been "giving the sack" to lovers with whom they choose not to consort.

Don't Care a Tinker's Dam

"Tinker's dam" refers to something of little value and most humble origin.

Long before the days of "wear-ever aluminumware" pots, kettles, and pans wore out so frequently that there sprang up a group of itinerant workers who named themselves tinkers, from the noises they made when at work. These tinkers traveled from town to town repairing pots, pans, and kettles. Their equipment included clay, which was used to make a mold or "dam" to retain melted solder against the joints of the articles they repaired. After the solder set, the dam of clay was worthless and thrown away. So from the lowly tinker of old we get today's impassioned "I don't care a tinker's dam."

At My Uncle's
and
Up the Spout

Almost from the beginning of time, the pawnbroker has been a social institution. And in the days when pawned merchandise consisted of anything of value, every pawnshop was equipped with an "uncus." This was a large hook used to pull pledged goods in and out of storage compartments. The word sounded so much like *uncle* that when they referred to an article left with the pawnbroker as security for a loan, people said the item was "at my uncle's."

Over time pawnbrokers began to find the "uncus" awkward and devised instead a "spout" by which pawned goods were carried aloft for overhead storage. When the pawned item was redeemed, it was brought down from the storage compartment via the "spout" and returned to the borrower. From this practice, the common phrase "up the spout" came to mean "pawned goods," and "down the spout" meant "redeemed property."

Hit a Snag

In American lumber camps a "snag" is a tree trunk fixed firmly in the bottom of a river, just barely protruding from the surface. These trunks are the bane of a lumberjack's existence. If you "hit a snag" while driving logs downstream, it jams up the rolling of the cut timber. What's more, until the snag is removed, no progress can be made.

Fly Off the Handle

This phrase originated in the backwoods of antebellum America when wood chopping was a necessity, and it had to be done by hand with an ax. Each ax had a long smooth handle, and unless the woodsman held on to the handle tightly at all times, the ax would "fly off the handle." From this frequent experience, colonial woodsmen came to call outbursts of bad temper "flying off the handle."

Cut and Dried

When something is simple or easy to explain, we say it's "cut and dried." For this expression, we are once again indebted to the lumber trade.

Wood, among lumbermen, is not lumber until it has gone through two processes. First it is "cut"; after cutting it is "dried." Only then is it lumber, ready for sale and use.

Clear Out for Guam

To set out on a journey without a planned destination is to "clear out for Guam." The expression originated long before the tiny Pacific island of Guam became strategically important during World War II.

When the Australian gold rush was at its height, many vessels left England for Australia loaded with prospectors but without arrangements for return cargoes. Naturally, the captains of these ships wanted to increase their profits by finding return cargo, but when leaving Sydney, they were required by customs regulations to name the outward ports for which they were bound. Since they were headed for *any* port with a return cargo, the captains would say that they were "clearing out for Guam," a catchall phrase that now refers to a journey with an unknown destination.

Fool's Gold

This expression serves as a warning to those who are bent upon wild-goose chases for wealth or who believe they can get something for nothing.

Shortly after Jamestown was settled and the colony of Virginia established, tales drifted back to England that gold existed in the hills of Virginia's Shenandoah country. Spurred by these wondrous accounts, a group of English miners departed for Virginia. When they arrived, they struck out for the golden hills and struck what they thought was gold. They sent a boatload of the ore back to England, but when it arrived at the London Company, a close examination revealed that instead of gold the miners had struck pyrite, a byproduct of iron and copper smelting that was called "fool's gold" by the ancient Greeks. The exasperated London Company officials, in response to the miners' demands for payment, sent a curt reply instead of money: "Beware of fool's gold."

Ever since, this phrase has been good advice for those who pursue claims of easy wealth.

See How It Pans Out

This phrase originated from gold mining. Miners still separate the coveted gold dust and nuggets from the sand in which they are found with a pan of water. When the pan is shaken, the heavier gold dust collects at its bottom. The lighter sand sifts through and floats off. From this practice the world has learned to discriminate in the same way the gold miner does—by "seeing how it pans out."

Piker

To be a "piker" is to be petty, cheap, and a poor sport. But where did the term originate? We have two answers from two different countries.

In England the expression alluded to a tramp or vagrant who aimlessly traveled the early English highways, which were called turnpikes. Those roaming the roads were dubbed "turnpikers," later shortened to "pikers."

In the United States, soon after gold was discovered in California, a group of undesirable men from Pike County, Missouri, emigrated to gold country. They were notorious for their crooked gambling, petty larcenies, and antisocial conduct. When their place of origin became known, they were nicknamed "pikers"—a term most unfair to other residents of Pike County, who were glad to be rid of their undesirable element.

Chinaman's Chance

Although this phrase, which refers to the odds being stacked heavily against success, is no longer commonly used, its origin is still of historical interest. The first literary reference to it is found in Bret Harte's comic poem *Plain Language from Truthful James*, commonly known as *The Heathen Chinee*. Harte, considered the father of the local-color school of writing, picked up the phrase from his fellow campers when he briefly tried his luck as a gold miner.

In the gold-mining camps of the West there was always at least one cook, who was usually Chinese. Generally he was the lone Asian at the camp and had few if any friends. Whenever the cook got into trouble with the law (which happened frequently and unfairly), unless he had a friend in the court, he had no chance of acquittal. As a result, miners developed the expression "not a Chinaman's chance."

Other sources believe that claims officials denied the Chinese their right to stake a claim for a gold mine if the mine was known to be of value; they had a "Chinaman's chance"—that is, none—of registering such a claim.

Beeline

In mathematics the shortest distance between two points is a straight line. The busy bee knew this elementary rule long before mathematics was known to humankind.

If you've ever watched a honeybee at work, you've seen that after loading itself up with nectar, it flies back to the beehive in a straight and direct line to drop it off. When people observed the industrious yet parsimonious habits of bees, the term "beeline" was born.

To a T

If you want your clothes to fit properly, you must be fitted "to a T." Why a "T"?

The answer is found in civilized people's first skilled trade—carpentry. When homes were first constructed from timber, woodcutters observed the importance of joining one piece of timber to another at proper angles and in symmetry. This created a need for an instrument that could be used to make angles true, perpendiculars straight, and parallels similar. Through a process of trial and error a simple instrument was devised, formed in the shape of a T with a crosspiece at one end. Because of its shape, this instrument was called a T-square. Soon anyone who wanted to signify perfection or precision used the phrase, "to a T."

Nest Egg

Your savings are commonly called your "nest egg."

Soon after the chicken was domesticated, farmers observed that hens had to be coaxed into prolific egg laying. They hit upon the idea of keeping an artificial egg in every hen's nest. This faux egg, called a "nest egg," helped the farmer make more money, which he could save as opposed to spend. Farmers thus began to call such planned savings their "nest eggs."

Eat Crow

To accept the humiliation of defeat is to "eat crow." This expression arose from the intense hatred farmers have long had toward the black crow—which, if not scared away from spring cornfields or from newly seeded wheat fields, will yank the plants right from the ground and eat the kernels or seeds, cutting the farmer's yield by a tremendous amount. So when farmers had to face an unpleasant reality, they would claim that the experience was like being forced to "eat crow."

Another farmers' legend about "eating crow" goes as follows:

An army private on leave went hunting. He shot down a tame crow, and placed his gun against a tree. The crow's owner happened to come along just as the bird fell to the ground.

The owner of the dead crow grabbed the gun and pointed it at the private. "Eat the crow or die," he said. When the soldier had eaten about half of the bird, the owner relented and returned the gun to him.

The private pointed the gun at the crow's master and ordered, "Now you eat the rest of the crow or die."

Led by the Nose

Someone easily influenced or who unwittingly follows the leadership of another is said to be "led by the nose." Of course this is being kind—because we could call the same person a dumb ox and be historically correct!

An ancient practice of farmers was to insert rings through an ox's nose. This way they could lead the ox to market without any hassle.

While on the subject of noses, the expression "counting noses" came from horse dealers, who did indeed count horses by counting their noses.

Jack of All Trades

This common phrase is a shortened version of "jack of all trades and master of none." It refers to those who claim to be proficient at countless tasks—but cannot perform a single one of them well.

The phrase was first used in England at the start of the Industrial Revolution. A large number of efficiency experts set up shop in London, advertising themselves as knowledgeable about every type of newfangled manufacturing process, trade, and business. For a substantial consideration, they would impart their knowledge to their retainers. But when they were retained, it soon became evident that their knowledge was limited and of no practical value. Wary industrialists started calling these self-appointed experts "jacks of all trades and masters of none." These experts, alas, are still with us, and so is the phrase.

Called on the Carpet

Ask any employee who's been "called on the carpet" what the phrase means, and she'll tell you, "Severely scolded." Why should a carpet be the symbol of a scolding? The answer is found along the early American railroad.

In the era before railroads big-business executives in large, well-appointed offices were a rarity. Such perks—which we now commonly associate with our captains of industry—were generally reserved back then for royalty. Railroad presidents were the first business leaders to feel the need to "put on a front." Because he worked in a stock-promoted industry that depended on public confidence, the head of a railroad was given extravagant trappings—typically a large, thickly carpeted office equipped with heavy furniture.

Unlike the CEOs of today, these pioneering presidents actually had daily contact with their workers. When workers were called into the president's office, it was usually because something had gone wrong. With their heads held downward in deference while being reprimanded, the workers noticed the thick carpet, and a summons to the office soon became known as the dreaded "called on the carpet."

Wildcat Deals

A business enterprise without a sound foundation is called a "wildcat deal." The phrase is often used to describe risky oil-drilling ventures, and it dates back to the days when state banks, operating under state charters, issued paper currency.

Because of constant manipulation, the value of such currency was never stable, and the rampant abuse ultimately resulted in the outlawing of state bank currency. The notes of the Bank of Michigan, depreciated by money sharks, happened to be imprinted with a wild panther. They were nicknamed wildcat notes, and because investors "lost their shirts" investing in them, it became fashionable to refer to all sour and unsound business transitions as "wildcat deals."

By and Large

Perhaps the handiest phrase in the English language that expresses the concept of fullness is "by and large." It means "in all respects, totally, comprehensively, completely, all-told, and all-inclusive."

In Sturney's *Mariner Magazine* of 1669 is found the earliest use of "by and large" in its original nautical sense: "with and without wind." "You see the ship handled in fair weather and foul, by and large." At the time this appeared, a sailor could not qualify for a captain's post unless he convinced the boat owner that he was capable of handling a vessel "by and large," that is, when sailing both with and without the wind.

The first literary use of the term in its current sense appeared in *The Wooden Word Dissected,* written in 1707 by Edward Ward, an English humorist born in Oxfordshire in 1667. Ward was of humble origin and picked up the phrase from sailors along the waterfront close to his boyhood home.

Know the Ropes

Sometimes a phrase doesn't become common until many years after the custom that inspired it has disappeared. To "know the ropes," which means to understand everything there is to know about a particular subject or task, fits this description "to a T."

The sailboats that preceded steamships were constructed with masts that rose from the decks of the vessel to support the sails and running rigging. These sails were outfitted with ropes. If a sailor did not know how to handle "the ropes," he could not qualify for an important post among a crew. All ambitious sailors made it their business to "know the ropes," but it wasn't until after the sailboat gave way to the steamship that the phrase became a part of the common vernacular.

Walk Chalks

The oldest test for drunkenness is "walking chalks." If the subject can walk a straight chalk line, he is pronounced sober; if he zigzags, he's drunk.

Ever since vessels first roamed the high seas, sailors have been known for jubilant shore leaves. Captains thus made it their business to test their crew's sobriety just before pulling out of port. Two closely spaced parallel lines were chalked upon the deck. The sailors suspected of being drunk were required to walk between the two chalk lines from one end to the other. If a sailor overstepped the lines, he was pronounced unfit to take up his duties, with the extent of his punishment left to the captain's discretion. Sailors called this test "walking chalks."

Hit the Hay

A lot of people think that the common phrase "hit the hay," meaning "go to sleep," came from farmers. It actually came from sailors!

Before the advent of modern navies, every seaman had to furnish his own bedding. Sailing outfitters sold bundles of hay stuffed into coarse canvas covers for ship bedding. When a sailor went to an outfitter to buy his ship bed, which generally cost one shilling, he would ask for "a hay." So when a sleepy sailor wanted to tell his mates he was off to bed, he'd say he was going to "hit the hay."

Today sailors have regular cots and berths, but we weary landlubbers still borrow a phrase from the sailors of long ago to say we're going to sleep.

Give the Slip

To elude or leave someone behind is to "give the slip."

Originally seamen coined this phrase, which referred to a floating buoy left at anchor with a chain cable. These contraptions could be left behind until it was convenient to return and put them on board again. To fasten the chain cable, the nearer end was slipped through a hawse pipe. The name sailors gave to this task was "the slip."

In contrast to the noise made when weighing the anchor, "the slip" was a silent maneuver. Sailors soon began calling things done quietly and under the cover of dark "giving the slip." And when they wanted to leave a mate out of their social activities, they would "give him the slip."

Bitter End

There is a controversy right to the bitter end about the origin of "the bitter end."

Many centuries ago wine makers, upon tasting wine from the dregs at the end of a wine barrel, found it to be bitter. They called such wine "the bitter end" and later began to refer to drawn-out arguments or procedures as matters dragging on "to the bitter end."

Other evidence suggests that the phrase was nautical. The old clipper ships were equipped with "bitters," around which the inboard cables were wound. The spot where the "bitters" were fastened to the inboard cables was called by sailors "the bitter end."

As a side note, "bitters" were originally "betters," seen in the following passage from Daniel Defoe's *Robinson Crusoe*: "We rode with two anchors ahead and the cables veered out to the better end."

When My Ship Comes In

A daydream almost all of us have had is "when my ship comes in"—the day when a large sum of money or a worldly fortune of great proportions is realized. This mythical ship is usually tossed away by the rough storms of reality, yet small wealth may be gained from knowing the phrase's origin.

During the days when Bristol, England, was the busiest and most flourishing seaport in the world, local tradesmen extended credit to sailors' wives who made their home in Bristol. This credit was extended to the very day when a husband's ship was scheduled to return to the port of Bristol. Because a ship on which her husband served meant her family's livelihood, it became practice among sailors' wives to refer to their men's ships as "my ship."

When a sailor's wife went on a shopping spree, instead of saying "charge it," as is the modern custom, she said, "I'll pay when my ship comes in."

Pour Oil on Troubled Waters

Although there are references by Pliny and Plutarch to the soothing effects of oil poured on raging rivers, the phrase "pour oil on troubled waters" didn't come into popular American use until June 2, 1774.

On that day Benjamin Franklin read before the Royal Society of England a paper on experiments he had conducted during a sea voyage from America to England. The waters on this voyage were so rough that Franklin was unable to keep his candle steadily lit in his cabin. In desperation, he poured oil out onto the ocean. When he observed the waters growing calmer, he continued pouring oil throughout the entire trip. Franklin's well-received findings were then put into practice by mariners with remarkable success. This gave rise to the expression and formula for overcoming any difficult situation—namely, "pour oil on troubled waters."

So Long

When it's time to take our leave, we say, "So long." For this phrase, we are indebted to the natives of East India, and to the awkward language skills of English sailors.

When English sailors returned to England after their first voyage to East India, they brought with them an Indian salutation. The Indian word *salaam* means "good-bye," but the best the tongue-tied sailors could do with *salaam* was "so long." Before long, they had all of England mispronouncing *salaam* and "so long" became a stock phrase.

Roaring Forties

It is customary to refer to any locality that teems with activity and excitement as the "roaring forties." Many think this phrase originated during the 1940s, when big bands played raucous tunes in large ballrooms. Others believe that the expression originated in New York City, where New Yorkers refer to the busy section that includes Times Square and is bounded by Fortieth and Fiftieth Streets as the "roaring forties."

The phrase actually comes from the logbooks of Atlantic Ocean sailors, who noted years ago that the most perilous and stormiest part of the Atlantic crossing is the zone from forty degrees north latitude to fifty degrees north. Here the wind roars the fiercest and storms rage the wildest. The same is true of the zone bounded by these latitudes on the trip from England to Australia in the southern oceans. The first literary reference to the "roaring forties" appeared in the book *At Last,* written in the mid-1800s by the English novelist and clergyman Charles Kingsley.

Give a Wide Berth

To "give a wide berth" means to make a generous allowance for someone's infirmities.

Any sailor "worth his salt" will tell you that to anchor a boat safely requires a space at least double the size of the boat. This space is known as "a wide berth"; "berth" itself originally referred to the actual space occupied by a ship at anchor. As ocean and river navigation developed, this phrase became popular.

From the same source is also derived the use of "berth" to describe a sleeping room or compartment on a boat or a train. These "berths," though, only took up as much space as the size of an average person.

An interesting side note: "Big Berthas," the huge guns on World War II battleships, derived their name from the nautical meaning of "berth," because of the massive space required when a Big Bertha was discharged.

Taken Aback

To be completely surprised, even shocked, by an event is to be "taken aback."

In the early days of the shipping industry, it required great effort and skill to stop a sailing vessel quickly. It took even more effort to get it to travel backward, which was often made necessary by the sudden appearance of a reef or jagged rocks. The method most commonly used to sail backward was to shift the direction of all the sails suddenly and quickly—in essence, to turn the sails backward. This operation required the help of all the crew. Sailors called this emergency maneuver "taking aback," and before long they began applying this phrase to any surprising situation.

Ride in the Black Maria

Around 1825, when English sea dogs were wont to celebrate too militantly for the peace of the staid Puritan residents, there lived along the Boston waterfront a portly African woman by the name of Maria Lee.

When the shore-leave sailors became too difficult for the local constables to handle, they'd summon "Black" Maria Lee, for whom no sea dog was too big or too strong to handle. She manacled the salty inebriates and was named by them "Black Maria."

So great was the respect of the sailors for Maria Lee's prowess that when the British police van was introduced in England in 1838 it was referred to as "the Black Maria." The term was brought back to the United States by American sailors who had ridden in the "Black Marias" of London when, on shore leave, they had imbibed too freely.

Stormy Petrel

We call individuals who, by their talk and conduct, stir up furies of wrath and excitement "stormy petrels."

118

Any sailor who has roamed the seven seas will tell you that, in certain regions of the Atlantic, there are large numbers of a particularly wild seabird that looks very much like a chicken. It feeds upon the small sea creatures that rise to the surface during storms. For centuries these chickenlike vultures have been called "petrels." These birds are able to foretell storms at sea, and, because they attack their prey during storms, are nicknamed "stormy petrels."

Sailors, never at a loss for colorful phrases, took to calling troublemakers "stormy petrels."

Pull Strings

The political operator, typically portrayed as a big, fat, cigar-chomping man, might hang his head in shame if he knew how "pulling strings" (his chief vocation) became part of our everyday speech.

Its genealogy dates back several centuries to France, when the social rage was the marionette show; it was fashionable to entertain at exclusive soirees with a puppet show. Frequently the marionette play satirized official or royal goings-on. The most successful marionette shows were those in which the puppeteer put into the mouths of his tiny characters the most interesting court gossip of the day. To buy his silence, influential officials would often do favors for this puppeteer, who was called "the string puller." It wasn't long before the populace learned that the string puller was the man to see for special favors.

Even today the expression "pull strings" conveys sinister backstage activity.

Fill the Bill

After a delightful dinner, you might push back your chair and remark to your dining partner that the meal "filled the bill."

Before there were professional theater critics (which some would still say is an oxymoron!), dramatic productions were advertised by circulating handbills containing extravagant claims about the play's wonderful actors and intriguing plots. The job of the stage manager of the theatrical troupe was to "fill the bill" with reading matter that would entice the public to "fill the house." Theatrical people picked up the phrase and used it among themselves to describe their excellent performances.

Hold a Candle

The history of this phrase is both quaint and, "no pun intended," quite illuminating.

In the days before gas and electric lights, the candle was the primary source of indoor illumination. Theaters and other places of amusement were lit by means of huge torch candles that, while burning, were held by young boys or men. This job was generally relegated to those who, because of their deficiencies, were unable to obtain more remunerative employment. The work was menial, and those who did it were held in low esteem. So if a person were considered unfit even to hold a lit candle, he was considered totally incompetent.

In the Limelight

A lot of untalented people thrive on being "in the limelight." Perhaps it would be a good thing if these solipsists were exposed to the actual rays of light this common phrase alludes to.

At the turn of the twentieth century it was discovered that burning a stick of lime in the flame of a combination of oxygen and hydrogen gases (or oxygen and coal gas) produced an intense light. The first commercial use of "limelight" was in theaters, to illuminate the spot on stage where the important part of a play was being enacted, later referred to as the "spotlight." Today's actors relish being "in the spotlight," but less talented and more shameless people choose to be "in the limelight" to keep publicly conspicuous their coarse theatrics.

Steal My Thunder

Fact is often stranger than fiction. Because there is an actual historical record of a case of thunder theft, we benefit from a phrase that means "to fear being deprived of the benefits of our own originality," usually by a foul usurper.

Around 1700 there lived a famous playwright who also was an ingenious stage-property man. Among his most famous inventions was a machine that produced the sound of thunder offstage. Alas, one of his professional rivals stole his invention. So heartbroken was the playwright over his great loss that for a long time he wept bitterly, crying, "He stole my thunder."

Pull Up Stakes

A hurried departure, or a measured decision to change location, is commonly called "pulling up stakes."

The phrase comes from the practice of the ancient nomads of the Arabian desert. They stayed in one place no more than a fortnight and lived in portable tents, set up temporarily with the aid of wooden stakes. When the nomads tired of a location, they "pulled up the stakes" of their tents, folded them across the backs of their beasts of burden, and, with all their belongings, went on their way to a new location in the desert. The settlers of the American West who, in their covered-wagon trips across our continent, lived briefly like the ancient nomads popularized the phrase "pull up stakes" throughout America.

Land-Office Business

When we want to describe a flourishing and prosperous enterprise, we say its owners are doing a "land-office business."

This saying dates back to the days in American history when Uncle Sam, in order to develop the West, gave away land to anyone willing to build a homestead on it. If you wanted to become a landowner, all you had to do was go to the land office and register your claim. In some of the western territories, huge crowds gathered around the land offices to obtain the free property, overburdening the clerks, who became too rushed to efficiently handle their demands. The homesteaders never forgot these crowds, and soon whenever they saw a thriving business they remarked, "They're doing a land-office business."

Make Tracks

When we leave secretly for an unknown destination or with great haste, we use the phrase "making tracks," a distinctly American version of "pulling up stakes."

The phrase originated with the early American pioneers who traveled in covered wagons, often referred to as wagon trains. When a pioneer deserted a wagon colony, he would rig up his wagon under cover of darkness and depart, unknown to his comrades, to seek his fortune on his own. The only traces he left behind were the tracks of his wagon. From this came the expression "making tracks."

From the same source comes "covering your tracks," meaning "to leave behind not a single clue."

To Pitch and Pay

This phrase was derived from a custom of the ancient marketplaces of England, and is very similar to the way displays in a modern bookstore work today.

The custom was first practiced in the Old Market of Blackwell Hall in London. When Blackwell Hall was in its "heyday," the word used by the market men for the display of merchandise was "pitching." Each stallkeeper paid a fee proportionate to the amount of space he used for "pitching" (displaying) his merchandise. The pitching fee was paid immediately after the pitching space was measured by the superintendent of the market. The market men called the preliminaries of getting the market ready for each day's business "to pitch and pay." The phrase became synonymous with transactions requiring cash payments.

To Pay on the Nail

Have you ever wondered why we say a cash buyer is required "to pay on the nail"? It arose from an old practice of the Limerick, Ireland, stock exchange.

In the center of this exchange was a pillar with a large brown plate of copper, three feet in diameter, where all the deposits of security for all stock-buying transactions were placed. This plate was called the Nail, because once a buyer placed his security on it, both buyer and seller were bound to their transaction as securely as if a written contract had been executed. Stock exchanges in Bristol and Liverpool had similarily designed Nails, each the symbol of final cash transactions.

To Buy on Tick

To "buy on tick" means to buy on credit. This phrase originated in France.

In French *estiquette* originally meant "it is recorded." When credit sales were introduced in France, storekeepers were compelled to keep records of all credit transactions. This meant that a credit customer would not be given her purchase until a record was made of it; she had to wait until the bookkeeper reported an *estiquette.* Through common usage, *estiquette* was contracted to *tique.* By the time retail credit was established in England, travelers had brought back to England the French *tique* in the form of "tick." Hence, the first English retail-credit sales were called "sales on tick."

7
Grub

People think a lot about food. They use food in a lot of common phrases, too. A wishful thinker has "pie in the sky" ideas. A gold medal following a world-record time is "frosting on the cake." When a man covets another man's unwanted woman, a hushed remark is that "one man's cookie is another man's cake." When somebody's jealous of your accomplishments, you turn with pride and say, "Eat your heart out." And when we think folks are "off their rocker," we say that they're "out to lunch" or "nutty as a fruitcake."

Common phrases evolved both from culinary practices, such as "three square meals" ("swabbies" in the eighteenth-century English navy ate off square wooden plates), and from the things we eat, such as "he's an oyster" (a close-mouthed person), or "he clammed up" (stopped talking).

While few would want to eat a grub, the thick wormlike larva of a ground-living beetle, this word for "food" came from the act of "grubbing," or digging in the ground for potatoes. "Grub" was also an actual street in London where "down and out" writers, having "taken it on

Grub

the chin," "hung out" while awaiting another "shot in the arm."

Drunk as Blazes

If there are stages of alcoholic intoxication, to be "drunk as blazes" must be the final stage.

A saint of the Catholic Church, St. Blase (also spelled Blaise) served as the bishop of Sebaste in Armenia (now Sivas, Turkey) around A.D. 316. When the Roman emperor Licinius began to persecute the Christians, Blase fled, but was captured. For refusing to deny his faith, he was flayed with wool-combing hooks and beheaded. Because of the way he was martyred, he became the patron saint of wool combers. The Orthodox Church held a feast in his honor each February 11. The day was initiated by huge marching processions of his followers, called Blasers, accompanied by merriment similar to the annual Mardi Gras in New Orleans. On festival day every good Blaser was "in his cups"—so much so that they were collectively called "drunken Blasers."

Cook Your Own Goose

A particular monarch's desire to cook a goose dinner is how this pithy expression was born.

Eric, king of Sweden, was a mighty warrior who used a small army to vanquish enemy troops superior in numbers and equipment. When King Eric set out to subdue one particularly unruly province of his kingdom, his military scouts advised him against it, because of the superior numbers of his foes. He paid no mind. When Eric's foes learned of his advance, and knowing of the king's fondness for goose, they hung up a huge goose for the king's troops to try to shoot down as a joke.

The king's forces engaged in battle and dispatched their enemies with only a few casualties. Heralds of the opposition were sent to the king to negotiate a surrender. When Eric was asked his terms, he responded, "To cook your own goose." When the surrender was final, King Eric sent for the enemy's goose, cooked it himself, and consumed it with a victor's relish.

Goose Hangs High

How did a dead goose hung in midair become an accepted symbol of human joy and wellness?

In medieval England riding and hunting were national pastimes. One sport combined the two in a competitive game. A group of hunters on horseback would go into the woods and seize a live goose. The head and the neck of the goose were then well greased, and the goose was hung by its feet from the limb of a tree. The hunter who could pull down the live goose while riding past it at full gallop kept it as his prize. The starting signal was the cry, "The goose hangs high," which soon became a catchphrase denoting happiness. Among wild-geese hunters, it was the custom to select a goose from the catch and "hang the goose high" before the door of the hunter's lodge. That way, everyone would know what he was having for dinner that night.

Grub

There was also a belief that when geese honked while in flight near the clouds, the weather would be fair. Because of this superstitious belief, the ancients cried, "The goose honks high," when they thought good weather was due.

Takes the Cheese

This phrase is used whenever someone does something inappropriate; typically, it applies to an incident that results in someone being humorously embarrassed. It means the exact opposite of "taking the cake"—an expression that originated at country fairs, because the first prize in dance contests was a decorated cake.

Beau Brummel, a fashion plate of his time and best friend of the prince regent who later became King George IV of England, took social liberties with the elite. He came notoriously late to formal dinners and expected that the meal wouldn't start until his arrival.

On one occasion, the marquis of Lansdowne invited Brummel to a large formal dinner. The sumptuous repast began on time, and when Beau finally appeared, cheese, the last course, was being served. The marquis turned to Brummel, who was crestfallen because the party had begun without him, and said, "Here, Beau, take the cheese."

Gossips did a thorough job of circulating the phrase among the masses.

Stew in Your Own Juice

Otto von Bismarck, a nineteenth-century chancellor of the German Empire, popularized this common phrase during the French-Russian War when he exhorted his armies to fight until the French "stewed in their own juices." But where and how did it originate?

When meats were first roasted, ancient chefs, sampling the savory juices and fats, learned that dipping a roasting ox in its own juices added a delicious taste that whetted the appetite. "Let the ox stew in its own juice" was born.

Teetotaler

Someone who abstains from drinking alcoholic beverages is called a "teetotaler." A lot of people think this means that the abstainer drinks tea instead of alcohol. The term actually came from a game.

The old top-spinning game of put and take, originally called T-totum and often spelled teetotum, was played with a four-sided top spun with the hand. On one side was inscribed a T, for the Latin word *totum,* meaning "all." On another side was imprinted a P, short for the Latin *ponere,* meaning "to put." A third side was marked with the letter N, for the Latin *nihil,* meaning "naught." The fourth side bore the letter A, for the Latin *aufere,* meaning "to take away."

The luckiest spin was the T, for whoever spun a T took *totum* or "all." The game was named for this winning spin.

When a movement for the prohibition of the sale and use of all intoxicating liquors gained momentum in England in 1833, its advocates preached total abstinence. Their slogan was "total abstinence or naught," with both the "total" and the "naught" borrowed from the game of teetotum, which was very popular at that time in England. As a result, prohibitionists were nicknamed "teetotalers."

Grub

The first individual to be branded a "teetotaler" was Richard Turner, a leading prohibitionist, who stuttered very badly and ended his speeches by stuttering at the top of his voice the prohibitionists' slogan so that it sounded like "t-t-t-t-total abstinence or naught."

Devil to Pay

Surprisingly, the devil has little to do with this expression, which refers to answering for another's transgressions.

For centuries English saloon keepers and tavern owners gave their institutions striking names. Following this practice, the owner of a barroom on Flat Street in London, near the London Civil Courts of Temple Bar, called his emporium The Devil. Here lawyers congregated daily after court, some spending more hours at The Devil than at their offices, and even spending large amounts of their clients' funds. So great did this abuse become that the number of clients whose monies were used by their lawyers to pay The Devil for drinks became legion. The defrauded clients bemoaned the fact by telling their friends their cash had gone "for The Devil to pay." This lament soon became a colorful daily expression.

The phrase "gone to the devil" comes from the same bar. When clients called at the offices of their "spirited lawyers," they found them out, and were told by the attendant on duty that the lawyers were "gone to The Devil."

Three Sheets to the Wind

It's said of a man so drunk that he staggers and reels to and fro that he is "three sheets to the wind." This expression has nautical roots, but there are two slightly different versions of how it developed.

One version has it that on four-masted ships, there were times when only three of the four masts were rigged with sails. If a sudden squall appeared, the ship could then pitch and roll in the strong winds. So when men similarly pitched and rolled from too much drink, they were said to be "three sheets to the wind."

A second story, and perhaps the more historically accurate of the two, also pertains to sailboats. These sailboats of yore typically had three sails per mast, and attached to the lower end of each sail was a large cord called a sheet that was used to shorten or extend the sail. When the sheet was tightened, the sail became rigid; if loosened, the sail would flap and flutter. If all three sheets of the three sails were loosened simultaneously, the vessel would reel and stagger, and the sails of the ship were said to be "in the wind." Sailors, who have always had a jargon of their own, would say a staggering mate who had imbibed too freely had gone "three sheets to the wind"—like a ship with all its sheets loosened.

Bone to Pick

If somebody has a "bone to pick" with you, chances are she has a grievance she wants to discuss. This phrase originated with Sicilian marriage feasts.

When the festive wedding dinner was over, the bride's father would hand the bridegroom a bone and say, "Pick this, for you have taken on a difficult task." Then, in the presence of the wedding guests, the groom would "pick the bone" while the bride looked on in silence and humility. Through this ritual the groom would publicly establish his authority over his wife and household. By "picking the bone" the young husband was granted the right to be the final and sole arbitor of all differences that might arise between the couple during their married life.

An offshoot of this phrase is the political saying, "Give a man a bone to pick on," which refers to giving a hungry job seeker a position to pacify him. Typically, the post given is one that those high in the party ranks would not want for themselves.

Piping Hot

Quaint customs of the past are the source of many expressions in daily use. Today "piping hot" is used to describe the condition of food taken from the stove to the dinner table. It originated long ago with the daily practice of the village baker.

In addition to an oven, every village baker had a pipe or horn. As soon as the bread was drawn from his oven, he would fetch his pipe and blow a signal to announce that his bread was ready for sale. At the sound of the pipe, the townsfolk would hurry to the baker's shop for "piping-hot" bread.

Make No Bones of It

The expression, which means having no trouble with a task, comes from a time when fish and fowl were the primary meat staples. The many poultry and fish bones made eating difficult and irksome, and unless the bones in the fish and fowl were handled well by a diner, a meal would not be satisfying. So to "make no bones of it" was to debone a carcass so thoroughly that you'd have no worries at all of choking on the meal (which was a lot more common before the Heimlich maneuver!).

Drink a Toast

On festive occasions when a host offers to "drink a toast," usually to acknowledge someone special or a happy occasion, you raise your glass and drink in unison with everyone else.

There was a time, though, when, at the call for a toast, you were expected to pick up a piece of toasted bread, soak it in your wine, and then eat it. Remember this the next time you're invited to a party or a wedding, and bring along a loaf of bread and a toaster!

Eat Humble Pie

"To eat humble pie" originally meant "to suffer a social and financial reversal," and while the phrase had been discarded for many years, it reemerged during the Great Depression. Now it's more commonly used to describe the humbling and humiliating experience of being proven wrong when you were certain you were right.

While you'd have never found this dish at a restaurant, "humble pie"—a meat pie made with the heart, liver, and

134

entrails of a stag—used to be served in medieval England, and only to the servants of the household. It got its name from the Latin *ubulus,* meaning "little loins."

Keep the Pot Boiling

While this phrase means "to keep to the task at hand," it once referred literally to a cook's constant struggle to keep a pot boiling.

Before there were gas or electric ranges and microwaves to heat prepared foods, a homemaker had to keep a wood fire going day and night under a pot of water so that meals could be ready on demand. If the fire went out and the pot cooled off, it might take several hours before water could be reheated. So one of the homemaker's most important tasks was to "keep the pot boiling."

Table d'Hôte

A confusing choice often found at fancy restaurants is between "table d'hôte" and "table à la carte." With the former, your choice of meals is restricted, whereas if you choose an à la carte dinner, you can select from among a variety of offerings.

In France every inn used to have a large public dining room. Here the landlord of the inn was king, and as a rule he considered himself a connoisseur of fine foods and liqueurs. Generally, though, the innkeeper was rather arbitrary about what he served. He insisted that his patrons eat what he served when he served it, and that they sit at one large common table designated the "table d'hôte" (the host's table). It wasn't until after the French Revolution that diners overturned many established social conventions and were allowed the luxury of dining à la carte.

Upper Crust

The "upper crust" is a phrase commonly used to describe the wealthiest and most distinguished class of society.

In the age of feudalism, when a meal was a feast and a wineglass a tumbler, a loaf of bread was a yard long. This made cutting the crust a sizable (and important) task! To cut the "upper crust" was an honor set apart as belonging to the most distinguished personage seated around the board. If a lord was dining with barons, His Lordship cut the "upper crust" and retained it for himself. If only barons were dining together, the eldest baron cut off and kept the "upper crust." Whatever the social order, the "upper crust" almost never made its way into the hands of serfs or vassals.

Eat Your Hat

It may seem odd to say "eat my hat" when you want to blow off some steam. But the "hat" in this common phrase was actually an ancient dish called hatte, that enjoyed a brief and popular vogue.

Because hatte contained a lot of spicy condiments and was very sharp to the taste, "eating your hatte" was a test not only of your palette but of your gastronomic mettle as well. Only those of the strongest (and, it was once believed, most fiery) temperament could truly "eat their hatte" completely.

Grub

Hurry Up

Parents who constantly admonish their children to "hurry up" may be surprised this popular phrase was used for many years only by members of the restaurant trade.

Restaurants used to be constructed almost identically, with the dining room on the main floor and the kitchen below ground level in a basement. The headwaiter's task was to keep the food moving upward from the basement without any delays. To do so, he would continually shout down from the dining room foyer to the kitchen below, "Hurry up!" Before long people made "hurry up" a part of daily conversation.

8
Spring Chicken

Life and death, sickness and health, and, more recently, fitness and wellness occupy a lot of what we think and talk about. Human frailty is "part and parcel" of the human condition, and—not wanting to "go to seed"—we "blow hot and cold" on various health and nutritional practices to keep "in shape." Nevertheless, some of us are "sick and tired" of and others "rubbed the wrong way" by the recent proliferation of diet fads. We wish these health nuts would "cool their heels." But this is unlikely; "business will proceed as usual," with a wealth of useful common phrases at hand, as always, to help us say what we really mean.

In the Pink

This phrase means "in perfect physical condition" or "of fine mettle." Botanists may try to claim the origin of the expression, because botanically speaking "in the pink" means "in full bloom." Actually, however, its origin comes from

138

childbirth. When a child is delivered, its skin is a ripe pink until exposure to the air, when it undergoes changes in color and texture and loses its natural pinkness.

Sleep Like a Top

There's nothing more comforting than to "sleep like a top." Yet a top doesn't sleep. Or does it? It does when the top is not a child's toy and instead a mouse!

In Italian, the word *topo* means "mouse." Mice are sound sleepers. This is particularly true of field mice. Italians long ago coined the saying, "*El dorme come un topo,*" which translated means "he sleeps like a mouse." But when the phrase was adopted in England, the Italian *topo* was shortened to "top." So to "sleep like a top" is really to "sleep like a mouse."

All Agog

Somebody eager, perhaps even "starry-eyed," over a happy event is "all agog." The phrase "all agog" originally comes from "with all eyes goggling."

Practitioners of medicine noticed that when somebody was anticipating a great event, such as marriage, their eyes became lustrous and animated. This eye condition they called "goggling eyes," and when applied to a throng of people (they thought the condition was contagious!) they said the group stood "with all eyes goggling." The phrase was eventually shortened to "all agog." It was also noted that disappointment caused the exact opposite eye condition, referred to as "all aground."

Grass Widow

This phrase commonly refers to divorcées and to all wives separated (for reasons good or bad) from their husbands.

Hundreds of years ago in Europe the summers were unbearably hot—especially in the lowlands, where little grass remained and all available land was used for tilling crops. Husbands thus sent their wives and children up into hills, where it was generally cooler, for the season. The grassy uplands were also used as places for workhorses to graze, relax, and recondition themselves for future labor. When they sent their horses to the grassy uplands, the farmers said they had put their horses "to grass." Wives sent "to grass" were called "grass widows."

The phrase caught on in the United States during the California gold rush, when husbands put their wives "to grass," or to board with families, while they went to the diggin's.

Sham Abraham

In the Bible Abraham is one of the noblest of the patriarchs. He was so religious a man that he was ready to sacrifice his son Isaac. Yet the Abraham in this phrase, which means to fake an illness, is not a direct reference to the biblical character.

Years ago in London, there was a hospital named Bethlehem. Its various wards were named after biblical characters. The ward set aside for the mentally unstable (but relatively harmless) patients was called Abraham. Patients of this ward were given license to beg on the streets without police harassment when they were well enough to leave the hospital. Numerous impostors sprang up, however, who took to begging and falsely claimed they were patients from the Abraham ward of the Bethlehem Hospital. So to "sham Abraham" was to beg without a license. When all begging was outlawed, it became a neat catchphrase for feigning all types of illness.

Up to Snuff

A person "up to snuff" is someone in great condition both mentally and physically. The person is "in shape" or "fit as a fiddle." But this phrase has little to do with tobacco or the sneezing powder popular among royalty in the eighteenth century.

The "snuff" in this phrase is an Anglicized form of the Norwegian adjective "snu," which means "cunning, crafty, and shrewd." So how did we get the word *snuff*? The Norwegian word for snuff is *snuus,* and the two words *snuus* and *snu* are so similar that they were confused with each other.

So while the meanings are different, it's much better to be "up to snuff" than to be "up to *snu*"!

Down in the Dumps

This, and the equally common phrase "got the blues," means to be sad or depressed.

One of the great pyramid-building pharaohs of ancient Egypt was stricken with what we now call a nervous break-down. He experienced intense melancholia and died when he was unable to fight it off. His name was Dumpos. After his death, people suffering from melancholia were said to be "down with Dumpos's disease."

The Dutch language, whose history postdates the Egyptian Empire, includes the word *dompig*, which means "dull, low, and misty." This can probably be traced back to Dumpos of Egypt as well.

With a Grain of Salt

When we don't believe a word of what somebody tells us, we "take it with a grain of salt."

There was a time, however, when an ancient ruler thought it wise to put a real grain of salt into every drink offered him, as an antidote to any poison that might have been put into it by a spy planted into his domestic service by his foes. This ruler was named Pompey, the Roman general and politician who was defeated by Caesar and murdered in Egypt. Pompey was so meticulous about his ritual that he carried with him his own supply of salt. It is from Pompey's use of salt as an antidote that we obtained our figurative expression.

If you're wondering why Pompey thought salt was an antidote for any poison, in antiquity salt was as venerated as gold and thought to be a panacea. Salt also had other virtues, which is why it made its way into other common phrases.

Eat a Man's Salt
and
Above the Salt

Among the Arabs, salt is a symbol of friendship and hospitality. It has long been an Arabian practice to regard acceptance of hospitality as a sacred bond between host and guest that prevents the guest from ever speaking ill of his host. This compact was sealed by partaking of the host's salt. From this ritual comes "to eat a man's salt," a phrase that means "to accept a man's hospitality."

Likewise, "to be above salt" means that a position of honor and social recognition has been extended to the guest at the dinner table. Generally this was directly opposite the host, or "above the salt's" position on the table.

Bedlam

The *American Heritage College Dictionary* (third edition) defines *bedlam* as a "place or situation of noisy uproar and confusion," and lists the word's origin as the Hospital of St. Mary in Bethlehem in London.

The Hospital of St. Mary was founded as a priory (a monastery governed by a prince) in 1247. It was first located at Bishopsgate and later moved to Lambeth. As early as 1402, it was a hospital for insane patients, and in 1547 was given to the Lord Mayor Corporation of London and incorporated as the Royal Foundation for Lunatics. The English commonly called the hospital Bedlam (an archaic or medieval version of Bethlehem), and when they came across a scene of chaos or confusion like those they assumed happened behind the hospital's walls, they would say, "It's bedlam."

Bats in the Belfry

If someone appears confused or displays bizarre behavior, we might say he has "bats in his belfry."

This common phrase dates back to the time when the tallest building in town was the watchtower, or belfry. Frequently, bats in huge numbers would fly in and out of a belfry. People seeing the bats thought they flew in erratic and crazy patterns that made no sense. The phrase "he's batty" also finds its origin in this wild flying about of bats in belfries.

Gone Batty

"Gone batty," an idiom meaning that someone is crazy or even "off her rocker," is so similar to the "bats" in "bats in the belfry" that you may think the two phrases' origins are similar. In fact, they're quite different.

In the early sixteenth century many English physicians sent patients suffering from mental disorders to the city of Bath to bathe in its mineral springs, which supposedly had restorative healing powers. This practice became so commonplace that there arose the expression "go to Bath," which soon became "gone Bathey"—pronounced *batty* in many parts of England.

Gone Haywire

"He has gone haywire," another phrase synonymous with "going crazy," is an American expression for which we have our nation's farmers to thank.

When a farmer bales hay, he uses "haywire." The farmer knows how hopeless his work becomes if this wire gets tangled. What's more, he knows how disarranged haywire gets when a bale of hay is broken, and dreads nothing more than cattle getting entangled in it. If the haywire breaks, the hay goes everywhere, and a hard day's work is lost. It's likely that "gone haywire" originated after a frustrated farmer spent a full day baling hay into bundles—only to see his work wasted because of improperly knotted and tied haywire.

Run Amok

The word *amok* is of Malaysian origin. Malaysia is reputed to have been home to the first known opium addicts in the world. While under its influence, the Malaysian opium addict could lose control of the nerves and senses, often rushing forth with unsheathed daggers and shouting, "Amok, amok," which in Malay means "kill." It was common for an opiated Malaysian to kill several people while in such a state. This is why "running amok" refers to impulsive acts.

Sick as a Horse

When we feel ill and no remedy seems to work, we say we're "sick as a horse."

A brief look at the horse's anatomy reveals that its diaphragm is not a complete partition in the abdomen, but rather is perforated by the gullet, which is where the stomach is compressed by the abdominal muscles. When a horse is nauseated, its pain is many times that of a similarly afflicted human, because relief is extremely difficult. Of course ancient veterinarians were relatively unschooled in the horse's anatomy and could offer no remedy for a sick animal save time. So when people got sick and nothing seemed to work, they'd say they were "sick as a horse."

Kiss the Wound and Make It Well

When a child is bruised, a caring mother usually says that she will "kiss the wound and make it well."

This phrase actually has its origin with a snakebite. It was observed that a foreign substance entered the body at the point of the bite, and swelling, pain, and sometimes death shortly followed. Through the process of trial and error, somebody realized that the bite should be sucked so that the poison could be removed. The process worked, and before long this remedy was being applied to all infectious wounds. Soon certain people were credited with remarkable ability to heal wounds by sucking. "Kiss the wound and make it well" is thus a relic of one of our first medical procedures.

Dead as a Doornail

About four centuries ago the doornail was the most important accessory on the main door of a wealthy, high-status individual's home. Such homes had on the outer front door a large metal knocker that, when lifted, fell on a massive nail. The nail was almost as large as a plate and several times thicker. The resulting knell was loud enough to awaken the soundest sleeper in the farthest room of the house.

The huge nail built especially for this purpose was called a "doornail." Because the "doornail" was whacked so loudly that even a deaf person could hear it, if no one answered the door, it was assumed the house was empty or that the owner was dead! From this came our expression "dead as a doornail."

Gone to Davy Jones's Locker

We all know that anyone who is buried or drowns at sea is said to have "gone to Davy Jones's locker," a phrase that's as old as navigation itself.

A studious old salt will tell you that there never was a Davy Jones. Instead "Davy" is derived from Duffy, which refers to a West Indian ghost or spirit. He might also tell you that "Jones" is a corruption of Jonah, the prophet, who was thrown into the sea. "Locker" is seamen's terminology for the container a sailor used for his most personal and private effects. Put them all together and you get the "casket of the spirit of Jonah"—or "Davy Jones's Locker."

Sands Have Run Out

This phrase refers to an hourglass, a container divided into two sections. From the top half, fine sands run slowly through a small opening into the bottom half. The time required for the sands to run completely out is, in many hourglasses, one hour. The sands thus became symbolic of the passage of time; when they ran out, there was no time left, which is a relatively peaceful reference to death.

Let Her Rip

If you've ever been anxious to start on a new project, chances are you've said, "Let her rip." It may be surprising, then, that this expression takes its origin from an inscription on tombstones.

The "rip" in this common phrase is actually the R. I. P. found on tombstones, short for *requiescat in pace* (rest in peace). Religious people believe that death is but a beginning of a better life in the hereafter. This allowed R.I.P., itself an abbreviation, to become the "rip" of this common phrase referring to the beginning of something new.

9
Top Banana

Many of us "take a shine to" contests and games, particularly games of chance. While such games are generally rigged against us, and we must "have a screw loose" to play what is essentially a "shakedown" for our money, we continue to gamble no matter how often we "get the short end of the stick" or end up "taking a bath" by getting "fleeced."

Games of chance have given us many phrases that we still use today, even in cases where the game itself is no longer played.

Thumbs Down

If you want to reject an idea, you say "thumbs down" or turn your thumb down. But contrary to popular belief, it was not a pair of movie critics that popularized this idiom. What's more, "thumbs down" initially meant approval rather than disapproval!

A popular sport in ancient Rome was the gladiator contest. Gladiators from other lands were taken captive by the Roman Legions and forced to fight each other. The contest

149

150

had one rule—"keep fighting." The spectators were the um-pires. When a gladiator who had fought bravely was de-feated and the victor about to kill him, the crowd could sig-nal the victor to grant mercy. To do so, they concealed their thumbs within their fists, or turned "thumbs down," which in Latin is *verso pollice.* As long as the thumbs were up and visible, the contest continued and the defeated was van-quished.

Some visiting dignitaries confused the signals, and when they returned to their native lands they said "thumbs down" meant "no mercy for the loser." Because of this misunderstanding, "thumbs down" has come to refer to dis-approval.

Point Blank

To speak "point blank"—very directly—is French in origin and comes to us from the game of archery.

We all know that hitting the center of the target is the best possible shot. On the target, the center is indicated by a small, round white spot, which in French is called the *point-blanc* or, in English, "white spot." To hit the *point-blanc* requires a skillfully executed, straight, and true shot. When archery became a popular sport in England, the French *point-blanc* was adopted by English archers and became the "point blank."

Keep the Ball Rolling

The old English game of bandy, a forerunner of modern tennis, gave birth to this common phrase. In bandy a player needed to keep the bandy ball rolling toward the opposition's goal in order to win. At spirited contests the crowd would urge on its favorite with the cry, "Keep the ball rolling!"

Bandy with Words

To talk a lot about nothing is to "bandy with words."

This phrase also came from bandy, a game in which the opposing players hit a small ball with a paddle to and fro until one of the players misses. A miss is a default and entitles the opponent to score. "Bandy" came to mean "hit and miss," and because the game sometimes appears aimless to onlookers "bandy" ultimately became associated with idle conversation.

Fast and Loose

To say one thing and do another or to act in a tricky way is to be "fast and loose."

The curious thing about this phrase is that it was originally the name of a game played at country fairs in England around the year 1500. The game was played with a stick and a large, intricately folded leather belt. The belt was placed edgewise on a table, and the player given a stick. If the player succeeded in holding the belt "fast" to the table, he was the winner. The game operator could use sleight of hand to pull at the ends of the belt, however, so no matter what the player did with the stick, the belt would always be "loose." The game was nicknamed "fast and loose" by those who had been duped out of their money.

Left in the Lurch

To be "left in the lurch" is to be left behind. Because this expression is used so frequently to describe brides whose grooms fail to show up for the marriage ceremony, it's commonly assumed that a "lurch" is a corner in a church.

The "lurch" in this common phrase is in fact the original name of a card game known as cribbage, spelled "lurche." In this game the first player to score sixty-one won the round. If the winner obtained sixty-one before her opponent scored thirty-one, the opponent was "lurched." Anyone who lost by a "lurch" was left so far behind she had no chance of winning the whole game.

Aboveboard

To be "aboveboard" is to be honest, truthful, and trustworthy. So it may surprise you that the phrase has its origins in a gambling house.

At gambling houses a "board" is the table around which the players are seated. Dishonest gamblers were once wont to keep their hands below the board, and, when unseen, to somehow manipulate the game to their advantage. This practice soon came to the attention of the other players, and through their insistence, all players had to keep their hands above the board during the entire progress of the game. Players known for their honesty were thus called "aboveboard."

Four-Flusher

Why do we call a faker or a bluffer a "four-flusher?" Astute poker players know the answer.

In the game of poker five cards of the same suit is called a flush, and it's a good hand to bet on. Traditionally, poker is a game in which you try to outsmart your opponents, often by bluffing. Holding four cards of the same suit has long been the basis for bluffing other players into thinking that a legitimate flush is held. These four-card flushes are fake flushes, and they're referred to by poker players as "four-flushes."

Pass the Buck

To pass a job or a responsibility on to someone else is to "pass the buck." President Harry Truman, familiar with the phrase, often exclaimed that "the buck stops here" when he had to make an unpopular decision.

This phrase is as old as card playing. It comes from the ancient practice of the current dealer placing a marker, called a "buck," in front of another player as a symbol that he would be the next dealer. If a player wanted to shirk the responsibility of dealing, he "passed the buck" along to the next player at the table.

Cold Decked

Nobody likes to be "cold decked," because this common phrase refers to being cheated.

During gold rush days gambling was the chief recreation in boomtowns. Most of the games were not played "on the up and up." Many professional gamblers made the rounds of the mining camps, and they made the most of their money by slipping into the game a "cold deck" composed of either rearranged or marked cards. The deck was called "cold" because it was not warmed up, as was a deck in constant use. When a miner lost all his money in a suspicious game, he said he'd been "cold decked."

The Game Is Not Worth the Candle

One of the best ways to say an idea is worthless is to say, "The game is not worth the candle."

In the days when candles were the only source of light, a group that wanted to play cards at night at a card room or any other public place was charged with the cost of the candles used. Those asked to play who had no desire to pay the fee would say, "The game is not worth the candle."

Card games have contributed many other common phrases to our working vocabulary as well, including:

Card shark
Not in the cards
Cards up your sleeve
Put your cards on the table
Play your cards
Play into the hands of

Playing with the Mouth

This phrase means that you will make good on your debts or that you have good credit.

In Continental gambling casinos it was customary for the management to extend credit to a familiar player when he thrust his forefinger into his mouth. The dealer knew this action to be the signal for a loan of a stack of chips. If the dealer thought the player's credit was good, he would nod his head approvingly. Playing on credit thus became known as "playing with the mouth."

Let the Cat Out of the Bag
and
Pig in a Poke

The phrase "let the cat out of the bag" refers to revealing a secret. "A pig in a poke" means that you've bought something you thought was of value—only to discover that it's worthless. But why have we put these two sides of the animal kingdom together in one explanation?

Both phrases can be directly traced to England, when travelling country fairs were a source of high amusement for people who lived in small towns and villages. These country fairs were often breeding grounds for those looking to make a quick shilling or two off unsuspecting country bumpkins through skin games, shell games, and sucker games.

The word *poc* is Celtic for "sack," and 'twas the custom to sell suckling pigs at these fairs, the snorters being bought in *pocs* (later "pokes").

'Twas also the practice of hucksters to put cats in the "pokes" rather than little pigs and to sell them blind—that is, sight unseen—whenever possible. When the seller claimed that opening the bag would let the suckling pig escape, the smart buyer would insist upon opening it, thus "letting the cat out of the bag" before he bought its contents. But the naive buyer would often buy blind and, upon returning home, discover that the "pig in the poke" was really a feline.

Takes the Cake

Among the African Americans in the Old South, one of the highlights of the social season used to be the cakewalking contest. The contestants, couples of all ages, practiced for months ahead of time; some even went into training for the event. "Clodhoppers" had no chance.

In these contests a gigantic cake was placed in the exact center of a large circle. The couple who strutted around the cake most gracefully and ingeniously received, from the carefully selected distinguished committee of judges, "the cake." These contests brought out the newest dance steps, which quickly spread across the country. When the winners gracefully "cakewalked" past the judges, they'd revel in the judges' shouts of, "That takes the cake!"

Lame Duck and Buck Fever

Hunters are known for their keenness of observation. To this keenness we are indebted for our common phrase "lame duck."

When wild ducks are in flight, they marshal themselves into battalions that are triangular in form, each individual duck posing its legs and head horizontally. A duck that's lame or otherwise disabled is unable to keep its position in the flock's flight.

Hunters call these birds "lame ducks." Likewise, if a member of a hunting party fails to keep up with her fellow hunters or comes back without any game, she's called "a lame duck."

Deer hunters are sometimes "lame ducks" because they get "buck fever," an expression that refers to the weird feeling of weakness and loss of nerve that can come over you when you're about to do something for the first time. Often a novice hunter gets anxious and sweaty when first encountering a wild buck. Hunters jokingly refer to these heart-racing palpitations as "buck fever."

Barking Up the Wrong Tree

When you've planned to accomplish something by using a particular method and your plan is thwarted because you should have gone about it some other way, you've been "barking up the wrong tree."

Hunters have always used dogs to track the whereabouts of their prey. After chasing the game, the dog often thought it had traced the prospective dinner's flight to a particular tree. The dog would then bark up that tree. Its master would hurry over, but sometimes he would find no animal there. The dog had been, quite literally, "barking up the wrong tree." This happened with such frequency that the old hunters coined a phrase for it.

Stalking Horse

A front man acting for an undisclosed person is called a "stalking horse." Originally, however, a "stalking horse" was a creature of an entirely different stripe, and actually looked like a genuine horse.

Wild fowl will generally fly away in fright at the sight of a hunter. But one day a mounted hunter noticed that when he dismounted and moved a good distance away from his horse, wild fowl could be shot easily. When this became common knowledge, those hunters who did not own horses were convinced a fake horse could be used as a decoy and they met largely with success. The dummy horses used were called "stalking horses" because the hunters stalked, or hid, behind them when hunting fowl.

Get a Bad Break
Behind the Eight Ball

We get both these expressions from the game of pool. To "get a bad break" is synonymous with misfortune, while being "behind the eight ball" means to be put in an uncomfortable position.

To begin a game of pool, the balls are arranged in the form of a triangle at one end of the table. At the other end is the cue ball. The opening shot, or break shot, is at the triangle of balls. If the break shot puts the pocket balls in positions where they can be pocketed easily by the next player, it is called a "bad break."

In a common variation of pool, the balls are numbered and must be pocketed in numerical order, with the exception of the eight ball which must be pocketed last. If it is sunk prematurely, the player is penalized. That's why it's bad luck to be "behind the eight ball"; it obstructs a player's progress in pocketing the other balls in rotation.

Dark Horse

A "dark horse" is an unknown entrant in any kind of contest, and typically comes out of nowhere without fanfare, publicity, or record of past success. The phrase was first used in the early days of horse racing.

Sam Flynn, a Tennessean, was a horse trader, but unbeknownst to others he was also a breeder of racing horses. It was his practice to drive his workhorses to various horse auctions. But if there was a horse race in the same town as an auction, he would bring along with him one of his "secret" racehorses disguised as a workhorse. He would then enter it into the race quietly and bet heavily on it against the celebrated and well-known favorites.

One of his horses was particularly swift—a coal-black stallion that he called Dusky Pete. One day Flynn entered Dusky Pete in an important race at a country fair. The natives were betting heavily on the favorites. Flynn took as many wagers as he could lay on his Dusty Pete.

Just before the running of the race, Judge McMindmee, one of the field judges and turf oracle of the neighborhood, arrived. He was told jokingly by the local touts of the foolish betting of Sam Flynn. The judge, who knew his horses, recognized Dusky Pete at the starting post. "Gentlemen," he said, "there's a dark horse in this race that will make some of you sick before supper." Of course Dusky Pete won the race, and the judge's words rang prophetically true. After that it became customary at races and other contests to "beware the dark horse."

Let Her Go Gallagher

Although not as common as it used to be, the phrase "let her go Gallagher" can still be heard when quick action is required. This phrase became popular following a horse race.

Morgan County, Kentucky, famous for both its horses and its horse races, was the home of Judge Beaver, who owned several celebrated trotting mares. One day the judge entered his favorite mare at a trotting meeting; she was ridden by a man named Gallagher, a popular jockey. Some very noted horses were entered against the judge's mare, and huge sums were wagered on the race.

At the end of the first half mile the judge's horse passed under the wire "neck and neck" with another horse. The judge, who had wagered a neat sum upon his horse, shouted at his jockey, "Let her go, Gallagher!" The jockey let the horse's reins loose and won the race by twelve lengths.

Tout

The fellow who hangs around racetracks and "confidentially" gives you "inside dope" on which horse to back got his title, "tout," quite honestly. "Tout" is an archaic word (pronounced *toot*) that means "snooper."

When horse racing became popular in England, professional gamblers employed secret agents to obtain stable information about competing horses, which they would then write down. The gamblers would then offer to sell these "tout" sheets for a premium to those looking for a winning advantage.

In the Soup

To be "in the soup" is to be in an unfortunate predicament.

In 1888 a boisterous group of boxing fans went to New York Harbor in a tugboat to welcome back their fight idol, Kilrain, from a successful tour of Europe. The group was inebriated, and the captain of Kilrain's boat, sensing trouble, would not let them board his vessel. A few tried anyway, and one fell overboard from the tug. Excitement followed, and when a reporter on the scene asked what had happened, the group replied that one of their members was "in the soup." The reporter used this phrase in a news story about the event, and the public picked up on it.

Later that same year the Chicago baseball team, as a publicity stunt, wore full dress suits instead of their uniforms. One spectator called the team the "Waiters," and after the first rally by the opposing team a fan cried out, "The Waiters are in the soup."

10
Kindred Spirits

 It was difficult to collect the common phrases in this chapter under one heading. While the majority arose from the house and home, others resulted from everyday people's observations of interesting things or events. So *Guinness Book of World Record* hopefuls take note: It's much easier to coin a common phrase than it is to balance a hundred wineglasses on your forehead!

Back Against the Wall

When you're in a tight spot and it looks like there's no way out, you've definitely got your "back against the wall."

This expression came from England. Back in the days before English streets had curbs (and before underground sewer systems), a typical street was one way with shops on only one side, a foot walk in front of the shops, and a wall along the edge of the foot walk. When such a street was crowded, the weakest were usually pushed "against the wall." Also, when there was a street fight (and in those days there were many), the winner would force the vanquished "against the wall."

A third story explains that when walking with a lady, a gentleman was to keep her to the outside of the wall, because it was along these walls that refuse and raw sewage would collect.

Sit Up and Take Notice

A teacher may tell an inattentive child to "sit up and take notice." This common phrase dates back to an Anglo-Indian custom that arose when the English first arrived in India and established colonies.

Shortly after a colony was established in Madras, any young lady who arrived to make her new home was received formally. At the reception she was attended by the master of ceremonies, who placed her on a high chair. There she was required to "sit up and take notice" of all the ladies and gentlemen in the settlement. Of course, once the colony had grown large this proved too great an ordeal, and it was soon abolished.

Nick of Time

Doing something at a critical moment is known as an act "in the nick of time." This phrase's origin is archaic; it dates all the way back to the days when a "nick" was a "nock," or what we today call a "notch."

Before clocks or pocketwatches, time was reckoned by notches on a stick. In those days, things happened "in the notch of time." With the evolution of "notch" into "nock" and then into "nick," the phrase took its present form.

Circle of Friends

The early Normans are credited with being the creators of open hearths for domestic use (and, as a result, of indoor heating).

Because the first open hearths, semicircular in shape, were crude and primitive, people had to sit very close to one to get warm. When the weather was cold, an entire family would gather in a semicircle opposite the one formed by the hearth, forming a complete circle. Only the immediate family used the hearth in this fashion, giving rise to the common phrase "family circle." Later, when others were invited to sit around the hearth, the phrase evolved into "circle of friends."

Hobnob

From their Norman conquerors, the English learned to use an open hearth for cooking and heating. At each corner of the hearth was a "hob"— a large container in which liquids were heated. Close to the hob was a small round table called a "nob" on which the "hob" could be placed for convenient serving. When friends visited one another, warm beer, which was kept in the "hob," was served and placed on the "nob." Friends sat cozily in the snuggery around the hearth, drinking, talking, and spending a pleasant evening "hobnobbing" with each other.

Come at Pudding Time

To "come at pudding time" is to arrive at the happiest moment. This phrase originated from the great significance bestowed upon puddings by the English, particularly during the seventeenth century.

Back then all English dinners began with a pudding. "Pudding time" was synonymous with "dinnertime," and if friends asked you to their home "at pudding time," you were being invited to dinner.

Now that pudding has been elevated to the high station of a dessert, "pudding time" has come to mean "happy or fortunate time."

Gift of Gab

The expression "gift of gab"—to speak fluently, if not endlessly—is of Scottish origin.

The word "gab" is Celtic for "mouth." So in this common phrase we have a rare example of the Scots giving away something for nothing (to be "Scotch" is to be extremely frugal). Of course the "gift" in this instance has no tangible value, which is why the Scots are so free with their "gab"!

Blue Blood

To think yourself a "blue blood" is to consider yourself of superior stock. When used as an insult, it means that you're a snob.

Spain was colonized by peoples descended from the Goths, a race with fair hair and light complexions. They were so fair that their bluish veins showed through their white skin, causing them to believe that their blood was blue. When the Moors, a dark people, conquered Spain, it was noted that no heavenly blue could be seen through their skin. Nevertheless, while they controlled Spain many a "blue-blooded" Castilian and Aragonian intermarried with the Moors. They intermarried at such a pace that when the Spaniards regained control of the country, the "blue bloods" were able to take charge and became the aristocrats and ruling party. The "blue bloods" held themselves apart from the masses and claimed a social superiority because of their fair skin and mythical "blue blood."

Blue Stockings

"By their blue stockings shall ye know them" was said of a group of intellectuals centuries ago. Today, to call people "blue stockings" is to call them snobs.

In 1400 a group of Italian ladies and gentlemen, hungry for intellectual discussion, formed at Venice a society called Della Calza. The group maintained a select Venetian membership until 1590, when most of the society moved to Paris; there it flourished under the name Bas-Bleu. The society was introduced in England in 1780, when a member, Mrs. Montague, started wearing blue stockings at her intellectual soirees from Paris to London. Before long all the members were wearing blue stockings. Prominent members included Benjamin Stillingfleet and Miss Mockton, countess of Cork, who kept the society going until her death in 1840. Because the society was always very exclusive, it became popular to call all snobs "blue stockings." The derisive expression "your mind is in your feet" also comes from the amused contempt in which members of the Blue Stocking Society were held by other scholars and thinkers.

Live Like a King

Most of us think the origin of this phrase is obvious. Kings have always lived lavishly, a condition any of us would envy. But for the real origin of this common phrase, we must dig a little deeper.

When Alexander the Great was waging his campaign through India, Porus, prince of India, was taken prisoner. Alexander had Porus brought before him and asked the prince how he expected to be treated. The prince was not easily intimidated, even by Alexander. Being a person of great wit, Prince Porus answered, "Like a king." Alexander was so impressed with the prince's regal reply that he ordered that Porus should indeed "live like a king"—and the two became fast friends.

Talk Turkey

Most Americans know that "let's talk turkey" is a request to get down to the business at hand. One story of this phrase's origin is amusing, but probably not true.

One of the original colonists, a Pilgrim, became friendly with an Indian hunter. One afternoon they went hunting and together bagged several buzzards and turkeys. When the hunt was over, they started to divide the spoils. The Pilgrim said to the Indian, "You may have the buzzards and I will take the turkeys." But the Indian knew his turkeys and declined. The Pilgrim, bent on getting the better of the deal, generously said, "I will take the turkeys and you may take the buzzards." But the Indian couldn't be fooled. "You never once 'talk turkey' to me." The Indian broke the stale-mate, and we have been "talking turkey" ever since.

It's more likely that this phrase evolved from early turkey hunters who imitated the turkey calls to attract the birds to where they were waiting with their hunting rifles. The hunter who "talked turkey" the best "bagged" the most turkeys.

Don't Give a Picayune

There is no better way to express anger, short of profanity, than to say, "I don't give a picayune."

A "picayune" is an old Piedmont coin worth about the same as a penny. Prior to 1857 it enjoyed considerable use in Louisiana. It had the same value as the fipenny bit in Pennsylvania or the fip in Virginia. In New England its equivalent was a fourpence haypenny, and in New York it was worth a sixpence. When currency and coins were stan-dardized, the picayune became worthless, and gave way to the nickel.

Dumb as a Dodo

Picture a bird the size of a grown bulldog, with wings as small as a bat's but unable to fly, bright yellow and clumsy feet, a hooked black nose almost as big as one of its feet, and an ex-pressionless gaze—and what you have is a dodo.

The dodo, thought to be a cross between a wild turkey and a pigeon, lived on the island of Mauritius in the Indian Ocean. Island settlers, finding no use for it for either food or utility, called it a "dodo bird" because of its "deadpan"

look. It became extinct during the seventeenth century because of its inability to fly away and escape when shot at,
leading many to think it was too dumb to run away from
danger. So we are left with the phrase "dumb as a dodo"—
even though it's we humans who stupidly extinguished a
species that offered no help to us, and no reason to fear it.

Kill with Kindness

While some still debate the merits of Darwin's theory of
evolution, there can be no debate that our common phrase
"killing with kindness" comes to us from a timeworn practice of the ape.

When a mother ape is overjoyed with the process of giving birth, she repeatedly embraces her newborn baby apes.
Often this affection, which comes from the arms of a very
large animal, is dangerous: The mother may crush or suffo-
cate her babies to death.

Get Up Your Dander

There is no connection between the words "dander" and
dandruff, just as there is no connection between anger and
the human scalp, unless you're referring to the old practice
of scalping your enemies. To "get up your dander" was
originally to "get up your damned anger" or to "see red."

How "dander" became a contraction for *damned anger*
is somewhat of a mystery. Some say that because of diffi-
culties pronouncing the word *damned* and the frequency of
their combined use, *damned* and *anger* were slurred into the
singular "dander." The latter word also had an advantage in

polite society as a much more respectable option. Many a mother has instructed her child to substitute "heck" for "hell" when cursing (unaware that the two words actually refer to the same thing; Hecate was the ancient Greek queen of Hades and protector of witches, and is by some credited as the source of "heck").

Psychiatrists call such word combinations neologisms—combinations sometimes uttered by schizophrenic patients. Perhaps we owe this expression to the mentally ill!

Dead Herring

A colorless personality or one with no zest for life is called a "dead herring."

Fishermen have known for centuries that as soon as a herring is taken out of the water, it dies. In fact, very few fishermen have ever seen a live herring, as only a rare and phenomenal herring will struggle to become unhooked. So fishermen coined the phrase, which can now apply to both fish and people, "dead herring."

The Four Hundred

Why are the socially elite called "the Four Hundred"? There are two different stories about the origin of this phrase, both attributed to Ward McAllister, the wealthy nineteenth-century arbiter of high society. We prefer the one that indirectly makes George Washington responsible!

In New York City around the year 1889 a group of fashionable citizens decided to celebrate the centenary of Washington's first presidential inauguration in a grand manner.

Wanting this celebration to be the social event of the year, they invited only the most prominent. In response to a question from a *New York Tribune* reporter about the guest list, McAllister remarked, "There are only four hundred persons in fashionable New York society." His quote was highly publicized, and the phrase "the Four Hundred" has been in use ever since.

Spirited Away

When people disappear without a trace, we say they've been "spirited away."

This phrase came into common use during the height of the African slave trade. The captains who operated the boats and trapped Africans by the foulest means possible were called "evil spirits" by their slaves. When these abducted slaves' families discovered they were missing, they were said to have been "spirited away" by the "evil spirits." Because kidnapping was the method used to catch slaves, "spirited away" became applicable to all forms of sudden disappearance.

Laugh Up Your Sleeve

This phrase refers to stifling a laugh or laughing discreetly even when the urge to laugh is strong.

Turn back the pages of history about three centuries. If your text is illustrated, you will find that all the leading men of the period wore coats that featured flowing sleeves with lace ruffles on the cuff. By raising his arm, a courtier could cover his entire face with his coat sleeve. That is exactly what he did when confronted with a tragically comic situation, and literally "laughed up his sleeve."

Spoke in the Wheel

When someone tries to detract from the pleasure of another or curtails another's enthusiasm, we say, "Don't put a spoke in the wheel."

When carriages were the chief means of getting around, it was common to insert an extra spoke in one of the wheels to act as a brake. This would prevent a carriage going downhill from getting out of control. So this common phrase literally says, "Don't put a brake on my good time." Whether anyone in a runaway carriage going quickly downhill ever actually had a good time is another matter altogether.

Peg Away

To "peg away" is to keep at a task without letup until it's finished.

Every party of traveling pioneers carried a tent as necessary equipment. Just before darkness fell, the tent would be hauled out and all hands would aid in setting it up for the night. But before the tent could be erected, pegs had to be hammered into the ground to hold the tent ropes. Because the ground was often rocky, this could actually be more difficult than raising the tent itself. The work also had to be done thoroughly and quickly, because the women and chil-

174

dren were waiting to get out of the cold night air. A back-slider caught shirking at the "pegging" task would be either reproached or encouraged by his fellow pioneers with the phrase "keep pegging away."

Dixie, Way Down in Dixie

The Great American Anachronism in Song, "Dixie, Way Down in Dixie," has an interesting history, particularly because most people think the phrase "way down" refers to the Deep South. Actually, "way down" in the popular folk chant refers to a valley in New York!

When the abolition movement started in New York State, about thirty-five years before the Civil War, there was a wealthy New York farmer whose name was Dixie. Knowing that slave ownership was becoming unpopular in his vicinity, he sold all his slaves, mostly to slaveholders in mountainous Shenandoah County. Dixie had been very good to his slaves, and those who were unfortunate enough to end up with cruel new taskmasters began to yearn for a return to Dixie's farm. Being in mountainous country, they prayed to be back "down in Dixie," because Dixie's land was in a valley. Their prayers became a chant, then a folk song, and now a saying of all people who wish they were back in the Old South.

Hurly-Burly

It's very easy to think that "hurly-burly"—a state of chaotic confusion—came into use (and was defined) because of the rapid jumbling sound the words make when said in tandem. Its origin actually lies in England.

There, a long time ago, lived two feuding families named Hurleigh and Burleigh. Their long feud kept their section of England in a constant state of violence, contest, and confusion. So great was the din they stirred up that adjoining country folks referred to that tumultuous region as "Hurleigh-Burleigh"—later shortened, like many common phrases, to its present spelling.

Gretna Green Marriages

For several centuries eloping couples running off in the middle of the night to start a new life together were said to have gotten "Gretna Green marriages." This phrase comes from the tiny hamlet of Gretna, Scotland.

In England it was both law and custom that no marriage could be solemnized without a license or a priest. But up to 1856, no such legal or canonical niceties were required in Scotland. All that was necessary was a mutual declaration of each party's willingness to marry before a single witness.

Gretna is the first Scottish town across the border between England and Scotland, and on the outskirts of town there was a blacksmith shop surrounded by a large field where horses grazed while waiting to be shod. The blacksmith was generally the first person the runaway lovers saw in Gretna and usually the witness to the declaration of marriage. Hasty elopers would find him tending the horses on the green and would shout to him their words of declaration without stopping or even getting out of their carriages. These marriages were called "Gretna Green marriages," a name that still applies to couples who elope.

Castle in Spain

If you've ever dreamed about obtaining a fabulous fortune, you've probably said, "Someday I'll have a castle in Spain."

In the eleventh century the Moors controlled Spain, and many French adventurers went there to seek their fortune. If a man struck it rich he stayed there, but if he was unsuccessful he returned to France and, to save face, told wondrous and imaginary tales of his acquired fortune, which often included a "castle in Spain." With this beguiling talk, our adventurer would woo French girls of rich parents. It was usually after the wedding that the rogue would confess that there was no "castle in Spain"—unless of course the girl's father bought them one as a "honeymoon" present.

Wear Soup and Fish

The old adage "The best way to a man's heart is through his stomach" certainly rings true in this common phrase that's probably more familiar to your grandparents than it is to you. At gala dinners soup and fish were commonly served before the main course. But to sit at the table, every man would have to wear a tuxedo or similarly appropriate evening clothes. So wearing a tuxedo or a handsome suit became "wearing soup and fish" whether you were invited to a fine meal at a formal dinner party or not.

Happy Hunting Ground

In addition to maize (corn), the American Indian has given us a few common phrases that we have incorporated into our daily vocabulary. Among these is "happy hunting ground."

To the male Indian, or brave, "happy hunting ground" is synonymous with "heaven." One of the brave's chief interests in life was hunting. Through it, the tribe was sustained. The brave's concept of paradise was thus a huge prairie full of game where he could hunt to his heart's content.

It was the Indians' spiritual belief that after death, the Great Spirit takes us to a bigger and better hunting ground. This is why when a brave was buried, his favorite pony was killed and buried with him, along with his bows and arrows. Fully prepared, the dead brave could sojourn forth to enjoy an eternity of good hunting.

Give Her the Gun

This common phrase of modern invention means "to put forth your every effort." It was coined by aviators and motor mechanics. "Give her the gun" referred to opening the throttle of the engine as widely as was possible, because the noise produced sounded like a gun firing.

Plug Ugly

"Plug ugly" originated in Baltimore, where, about one hundred years ago, there flourished a vicious gang of murderous thieves. Like all other gangs, it had a leader who, in the gang's regular meetings, gave out assignments and strict orders. At the end of each meeting, just before the gang set forth to do its dirty work, he would command his thugs thusly: "If day resists, plug 'um ugly," which in gangland vernacular meant to fill a victim's face with sufficient lead shot to make him "ugly"—or, more succinctly, "shoot to kill." When the gang was finally apprehended, they were described in a newspaper article as the "Plug Uglies."

It's Not Worth a Rap

To Irish pocketbooks we must go for the meaning of "not worth a rap."

In 1721 there was a great scarcity of small-denomination coins. So acute was this shortage, and so depressed were economic conditions, that the Irish Mint circulated a new coin called a "rap" whose worth was half of a farthing, or the equivalent of one-sixteenth of an American penny. Items of little value have since been referred to as "not worth a rap."

Born to the Purple

Any individual born into a position of great wealth or exalted station is "born to the purple." It is not without reason that the color purple symbolizes great power and riches. Like gold and diamonds, purple was once a rarity.

At one time there was only one source of purple dye: a rare species of shellfish found only in the Tyrian waters of the Mediterranean. From the adrenal glands of these mollusks came the first purple pigments. Because only small amounts of the dye could be obtained from large amounts of shellfish, these amounts were claimed by the head of the Italian government as his own to color his regal garments.

To Play at Ducks and Drakes

We derive this common phrase, which refers to loose spending and foolish money squandering, from the child's game of ducks and drakes. The game involves skipping flat stones across the surface of a pond and noting the rippling effects, similar to those produced by ducks and drakes when they take off from the water.

In the year 1585 a group of English noblemen who had been out late carousing played the game in the moonlight—but instead of stones they used coins. When the townsfolk heard of this wasteful use of money, they called the noblemen's game "playing at ducks and drakes."

Oh Yes!

This phrase—everyone is familiar with its meaning—was acquired from a very old practice.

"Oh yes!" is a contraction of *oyez,* French for "hear ye." It was the cry, *"Oyez! Oyez! Oyez!"* from the first French town criers that let everyone know they were about to make a public announcement or read a public proclamation. In many jurisdictions to this day, the opening session of civil and criminal courts starts with the bailiff saying, "Hear ye! Hear ye! Hear ye!" Our "oh yes!" is a contraction of the ancient *oyez!*

11
To Make a Point

In our final chapter we list those phrases that can be attributed to a single person, and those that did not fall into a previous category.

Life of Riley

To live the "life of Riley," among Americans, is to have no work, good food, and not a worry in the world. There are two explanations for this common phrase.

Some say that the "Riley" referred to is none other than the great Hoosier poet James Whitcomb Riley. True, he wrote *Little Orphant Annie, The Raggedy Man,* and other famous poems, including the comic verse "When the Frost Is on the Punkin," all of which have become famous phrases on their own. Nevertheless, some say that he was one of the laziest men ever to come out of Indiana.

Before his recognition as a poet, his neighbors often wondered about him. He left school at sixteen and occasionally worked odd jobs. He often appeared in the streets of Greenfield, Indiana, more than slightly inebriated, indulging himself with many a lark and spree. In fact, Riley was considered the town loafer. Mothers taught their children not to live the "life of Riley."

Others believe that the phrase originated with one Patrick Roony, a stand-up comic who wrote a little song in the late 1800s. A Mr. Reilly, a "stargazer" or dreamer, was the central character in the Irish entertainer's song. Mr. Reilly didn't amount to much, but he imagined what he would do if he were rich—how life would look at the top. Since many had the same dreams as Reilly, but didn't know the correct spelling of his name, they wished that they, too, could live the "life of Riley."

Neither Rhyme nor Reason

The harshest condemnation, however polite, of another's work is to say it has "neither rhyme nor reason." The odd thing about this phrase is that, when it was originated by Edmund Spenser, he was seeking payment for some poems he had composed for Queen Elizabeth. By his use of "nor rhyme nor reason," he obtained money long due him from the stingy monarch.

At the queen's request Spenser wrote for her a collection of poems. When he presented them to her, Elizabeth issued an order to pay him a specific sum. When Lord Treasurer Burleigh saw the order, he fumed, "What? All this for a song?" The queen replied, "Then give him what is reason." Spenser waited. After receiving no money, and with the queen still retaining his poems, he wrote her:

> I was promised on a time
> To have reason for my rhyme
> For that time unto this season
> I received nor rhyme nor reason

After receiving the poem, the queen commanded the practical lord treasurer to pay Spenser the original amount she had promised. Spenser received his money, and the world acquired "neither rhyme nor reason."

Bone Up for an Examination

To prepare for an examination can be called "boning up," but it has nothing to do with bones.

Some years ago there was a learned man named Bohn who, wanting to make life easier for Greek and Latin students, published literal translations in English of the Greek and Latin classics. These translations so greatly aided students that they nicknamed the translations bones. The use of the bones was called "boning up." Later Bohn's texts were called ponies and trots because of the speed with which a student could master his work with their aid.

Before You Can Say Jack Robinson

In the early part of the eighteenth century there lived in London an eccentric named John Robinson, popularly called Jack Robinson.

Jack was fond of appearing each evening at several places where he knew guests were being received. He would present his card to the butler and have his name announced, but before the host or hostess could receive him, he would be off to the next party. This scandalous act soon became "all the talk" among the elite.

When a London tobacconist named Hudson, who was also a singer and songwriter, heard of Robinson's antics, he put them into a song that he first sang at the soirees of the aristocracy. Later the masses picked it up, and to this day the phrase "before you can say Jack Robinson" enjoys popular usage as describing extreme haste.

Open Sesame

In "The Tale of Ali Baba and the Forty Thieves," from *Arabian Nights,* the doors to the robbers' den could be opened only by giving the command "open sesame." This tale was so intensely gripping to our forefathers that the magical phrase "open sesame" has become a humorous way to announce our presence at a doorway.

As a side note, the sesame is a rare Eastern plant used in ancient times for medicinal purposes.

Lick into Shape

When we are engaged in finishing a long project, we're "licking it into shape." When we use this phrase, we are actually repeating a primitive conception of how young bear cubs attained their body forms.

People used to believe that bear cubs were born as soft, lumpy masses; the mother bear then "licked" her offspring into shape and formed them. In the forward to Burton's *Anatomy of Melancholy,* published in 1621, we find:

> I was enforced as a beare doth her whelps to bring forth this confused lumpe. I had not the time to licke it into forme, as she doth her young ones, but even so to publish it as it was first written.

Ax to Grind

This phrase's first literary appearance was in Charles Miner's contribution to the *Wilksbane Gleaner* in 1811, titled "Who'll Turn the Grindstone." He stated, "When I see a merchant over-polite to his customers, thinks I that man has an ax to grind."

In this essay Miner related his boyhood experience of being duped, by flattery, into grinding an ax for a stranger until his hands were blistered. The incident impressed Miner so indelibly that as an adult, he set out to warn the world of the perfidy of flatterers. He wrote:

> When I was a little boy, I was accosted, one cold day, by a man with an ax on his shoulder.
>
> "My pretty boy," says he, "has your father a grindstone?"
>
> "Yes, sir," said I.
>
> "You are a fine fellow," said he. "Will you let me grind my ax upon it?"
>
> Pleased by the compliment, the gentleman's bidding was done by me, water being procured for him, and grindstone kept in motion until my hands blistered. The smiling gentleman kept up his flattery. Before the grinding was done, the school-bell rang and after the ax had the proper edge on it, the man

said, "Now you little rascal, you've played truant; scad to school or you'll rue it!"

Miner never forgot the incident, and when he saw one person flattering another, he said, "That man has an ax to grind." His essay gave the phrase wide circulation, and it became a true American idiom to describe people whose motives are not entirely clear.

Some sources credit Ben Franklin with inventing this phrase, stating that the story appeared in his widely read *Poor Richard's Almanac.* Did Old Ben borrow this story from Miner and claim it as his own, or did a well-traveled woodsman dupe both writers when they were young?

To Josh

To "josh" means to joke or make fun of, usually at someone else's expense.

Josh Billings was one of America's most celebrated humorists. He lived from 1818 to 1885. His writings were sharp, humorous, and witty, and he frequently mocked the goings-on of public officials, high society, and "bigwigs" in general. He was the first American humorist to become a best-selling author, and his name was known in every household. So widely read was Billings that it became the practice to say "to josh" instead of "to joke."

Keeping Up with the Joneses

A sad commentary upon twentieth-century American living is the obsessive suburban desire to "keep up with the Joneses."

This phrase gets its name from the title of a comic strip drawn by I. Bacheller and first published in 1911. So true to form were the characters of Bacheller's strip that, even though it is no longer published, its title, *Keeping Up with the Joneses,* occupies a rare position of prominence among American common phrases.

Confidence Man

A "confidence man" is one who, by winning your confidence through exaggerated claims of special knowledge and influence, gets you to part with your money on the promise that he will multiply it for you many times over. The phrase "con man" is distinctly American in origin.

The term was coined by the New York City Police after having been informed by numerous people that a very well-dressed man of exceedingly genteel manners had duped them. The man, in a very winning manner, had said to a number of New Yorkers, "Have you enough confidence in me to lend me five dollars for an hour or two?" Nevertheless, he failed to return the money at the time and place he had promised. All he left behind him was the title the police gave him, the "Confidence Man."

Tom and Jerry

The very popular mixed drink called the "Tom and Jerry" did not get its name from two bartenders whose names were Tom and Jerry. The source is instead Pierce Egan's *Life in London.* This famous novel features two main characters,

Corinthian Tom and Jerry Hawthorn, celebrated rakes whose sporting activities lead them to ruin.

Life in London was a best-seller of its day, and "Tom" and "Jerry" were on the lips of many in England. Soon the phrase became a popular nickname for the cheap and shady taverns of the type frequented by the two characters in Egan's novel. In these establishments, the most popular drink consisted of a hot concoction of rum and water mixed with cinnamon, cloves, and other spices. The drink was popular among Englishmen, and because it was first served in the "Tom and Jerry" shops it ended up with the very same name.

Dirty Work at the Crossroads

When we suspect foul play, often there's "dirty work at the crossroads."

The origin of this phrase is Walter Melville's melodrama *A Girl's Cross Roads*. As a small boy Melville had seen enacted the old custom of burying people who committed suicide at crossroads with stakes driven through their hearts. Melville, having an intense interest in melodrama, was impressed deeply by such burials. So when he wrote his melodrama the villainy took place at the crossroads, thus making popular the phrase "there's dirty work at the crossroads."

So This Is Paris

When someone is in awe of a spectacular sight, they might say, "So this is Paris."

The phrase first gained public prominence shortly after it was coined in 1765 by the English novelist and humorist Laurence Sterne. It appeared in his novel *The Life and Opinions of Tristram Shandy,* one of the eighteenth-century masterpieces of English literature because, unlike traditional novels that focused on external events, it revealed the thoughts and feelings of the narrator.

In the seventeenth chapter of the seventh volume there appears, "Crack, crack, crack, crack, crack, so this is Paris! quoth I, and so this is Paris! Humph! Paris! cried I, repeating the name a third time." Paris made such a deep impression upon Sterne during his travels that he returned to live in France for two years and later wrote *A Sentimental Journey Through France and Italy,* a work that records his appreciation of the social customs he encountered there.

Take Down a Peg

To embarrass or humiliate a conceited or arrogant person is to "take them down a peg."

The earliest reference to this common phrase appears in the writings of St. Dunstan (A.D. 925–988), one of the early archbishops of Canterbury. He tells a story of a group of Saxons quarreling over their cups, and his placing pegs into their huge drinking bowls so that when men drank from the same bowl, none could drink more than his share. Each drinker could only "take down a peg."

Drinking contests were also frequent at the time and were fiercely battled events. The depth of the drinking

190

vessels used were measured off by pegs. The contestant who brought the surface of his liquor a peg lower than that of his competitor was declared the winner. The loser was, well, "taken down a peg."

Among sailors, to "take down a peg" originally referred to the ship's colors when they were raised and lowered by means of pegs. The higher the colors were raised, the greater the honor. For the colors to be "taken down a peg" was a dishonor to the entire crew.

A-1 Condition

Unless we're sure a brand-new article is in "A-1 condition," we won't buy it!

Lloyd's of London was the first insurer of ships and cargoes at sea. Because of the great risk involved, Lloyd's did not insure every vessel for which insurance was sought. The company established very strict standards, and unless the vessel "lived up" to those specifications, insurance would be denied. If and only if a vessel met Lloyd's specifications for size and construction was it put on Lloyd's Class A list, and if its equipment was of the best quality it was called "A-1." In marine circles "A-1" quickly became associated with perfection. When Lloyd's became a general insurer of almost anything imaginable (including Mary Hart's legs and Jennifer Lopez's butt), it called safe risks "A-1s."

It is rumored that Lloyd's borrowed the system from the French who for years, as a precaution against counterfeiting, marked all coins made in the Paris Mint with an A.

Even today, if you want to say something great about a guy in French, you say, *"C'est un homme marqué à la A."* Roughly translated: "He's a man marked by an A."

To Be Dunned

"To be dunned" is to be pressed hard by a creditor for payment of a delinquent debt. This phrase originated from the works of one man, an English bailiff named Joe Dun. When entrusted with a court order for the collection of a debt, Dun seldom failed to bring the debtor to book.

So great was his reputation for forceful tactics that creditors would tell their debtors, "Unless you pay, I will have Dun after you." Before long Dun was an institution, and his name became synonymous with the collection of past-due accounts.

Annie Oakleys

An "Annie Oakley" is a free ticket to a public performance for which there is normally a price for admission. It gets its name from one of the ablest circus performers of all time— Miss Annie Oakley.

Annie was the headline performer of the original *Buffalo Bill's Wild West Show.* She was billed Little Sure Shot because of her astonishing accuracy with a repeating rifle. One of her feats was throwing a playing card into the air and, before it landed, shooting holes in all of its printed spots. When the card came down, it looked like a punched meal ticket.

It was the custom in those days to punch a complimentary ticket full of holes before it was issued to the lucky ticket holder. Because Annie Oakley's target playing cards resembled such complimentary tickets, it became customary to call all free tickets "Annie Oakleys."

Eldorado

When Columbus's discovery of America was finally accepted as fact, the story of his ventures filtered across Spain by word of mouth. Highly exaggerated descriptions of America accompanied the information that was passed along. One story that spread was that somewhere in the central regions of South America there was a fabulously wealthy city made entirely of gold. To give credit to their imaginary accounts, the talebearers named the city "El Dorado," which in Spanish means "the gilded."

We have Americanized "El Dorado" into "Eldorado" and use it now to refer to grandiose visions of wealth and fortune painted by high-pressure salesmen and other vultures who prey upon a gullible public seeking great riches through small investments.

We hope these common phrases have likewise provided a wealth of riches for a small investment, and trust that "Eldorado" is a fitting place to end our book.

Index

194